CAIRO PA
IN SOCIAL S

Volume 19, Monograph 1, Spring 1996

NILOPOLITICS:
A HYDROLOGICAL REGIME
1870-1990

By

MOHAMED-HATEM AL-ATAWY

THE AMERICAN UNIVERSITY IN CAIRO PRESS

Copyright (c) 1996 by the American University in Cairo Press
113, Sharia Kasr el Aini
Cairo, Egypt

All rights reserved. No part of this publication may be reproduced, stored in a retrieval system, or transmitted in any form or by any means, electronic, mechanical, photocopying, recording or otherwise, without prior written permission of the copyright owner.

Dar el Kutub No. 8265/96
ISBN 977 424 407 9
Printed in Egypt by the Printshop of the American University in Cairo

CONTENTS

ACKNOWLEDGEMENTS	v
MAP	vi
INTRODUCTION: TO LEAD OR NOT TO LEAD	1
CHAPTER ONE: EGYPT'S IMPERIAL ATTEMPT	5
African Players	5
European Control of Africa	12
CHAPTER TWO: BRITAIN THE MASTER OF THE NILE	14
Colonial Interests	14
The British-Built Regime	18
CHAPTER THREE: BRITAIN THE MODERATOR	28
The Interwar Period	29
Interests	31
The Regime	34
CHAPTER FOUR: EGYPT IN THE LEAD	41
Interests	44
The Regime	46
CONCLUSION: THE PAST, THE FUTURE	54
SELECTED BIBLIOGRAPHY	58
ABOUT THE AUTHOR	62

ACKNOWLEDGMENTS

I would like to extend my gratitude to the following people for their great help:

Mohamed Gad;
Dr. Salwa Gomaa;
Karim Haggag;
Dr. Jeffrey Helsing;
Amr al-Jowaily;
Mrs. Sohair Mehanna;
Dr. Cyrus Reed;
Dr. Mustafa al-Sayed;
Dr. Earl Sullivan;
Dina Zeidan; and
Sami Zeidan.

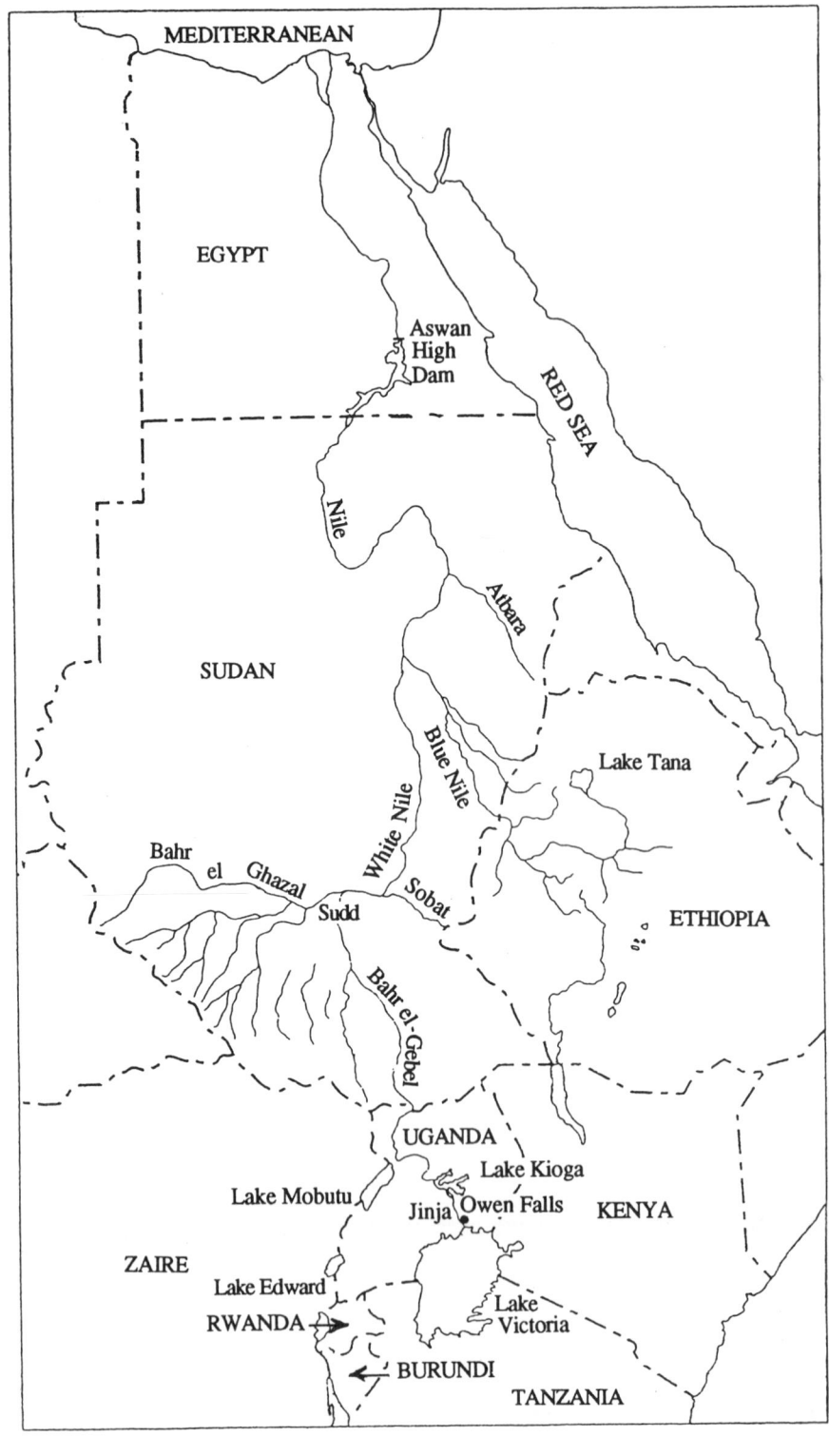

INTRODUCTION:

TO LEAD OR NOT TO LEAD

The Nile has a special place among the rivers of the world. It gave rise to one of the most ancient and sophisticated civilizations. From its earliest beginnings, Egypt was indeed "the gift of the Nile". This did not change with the coming of colonial powers to the African continent. Great Britain, which occupied Egypt in 1882, worked to secure Egypt's water needs through international agreements with other riparian states, or with the colonial powers occupying those states. However, with the growing developmental needs of other countries, notably the Sudan, Uganda and Ethiopia, conflict threatened relations among riparian states. This problem was handled through bilateral agreements between Egypt and other countries, as well as through the establishment of multilateral technical links for the riparian states, such as the Hydrometereological Survey Association.[1]

Egypt depends on the Nile for about 90 per cent of its water resources.[2] About 99 per cent of Egypt's cultivated land depends on the Nile water,[3] while about 35 per cent of the population in 1990 were involved in agriculture.[4] Moreover, about 97 per cent of Egypt's water resources comes from outside its territory,[5] thus adding to the sense of insecurity it feels vis-a-vis securing its water needs. Egypt's population is increasing while water resources are at best stagnant. Thus, it has been predicted that by the year 2025 the per capita share of water in Egypt will be 980 cubic meters

---

[1] Abdel-Malek Awda, and Hamdi Abdel-Rahman, "al-Ta`awan al-iqlimy fil-qarn al-ifriqi wa haud al-neel" (The Regional Cooperation in the Horn-of-Africa and the Nile Basin), *al-Siassa al-dawliya*, 132-44, April 1991, p. 162.

[2] Yasser Aly Hashem, "al-Ab`ad al-siaasiah wal-iqtsaddiah wal-qanouniah li-azzmat al-miah" (The Political, Economic an Legal Dimensions of the Water Problem), *al-Siassa al-dawliya*, 210-5, April 1991, p. 150.

[3] Butrous Butrous Ghali, "Idarat al-mayah fi wadi al-Neal" (Water Managment in the Nile Valley), *al-Siassa al-dawliya*, 116-19, April 1991, p. 116.

[4] Natasha Beschorner, "Water and Instability in the Middle East" *Adelphi Papers*, No. 273, Winter 1992/3, p. 5.

[5] Peter Gleick, "Water and Conflict", *International Security*, Vol. 18: 79-112, Summer 1993, p. 101.

per year, or less than the 1000 cubic meters per year required for Egypt to be an efficient, moderately industrialized nation.[6]

Other Nile riparian states are not in a much better situation. Although the Sudan is not currently utilizing all its share of Nile water authorized by a 1959 agreement with Egypt, the stipulated share is not sufficient to cultivate the vast areas of the country that are currently unutilized. The northern parts of the country, where the ruling political elite originates, depends almost entirely on the river because of its arid land. Other riparian countries are also expected to have increasing demands on the Nile water, again because of increasing populations that by 2025 will eventually reduce the per capita share of Ethiopia to 980 cubic meters per year, of Tanzania to 900 cubic meters per year, of Rwanda to 350 cubic meters per year and of Kenya to 190 cubic meters per year.[7]

Obviously, access to water is a major issue for the national security of Nile riparian states. This work demonstrates how water has affected the conduct of international relations among the states of the Nile.

The concept of "regimes" is useful in trying to understand relations among the Nile's riparian states. The definition of regimes adopted in this work is that of Stephen Krasner. He defines regimes as "sets of implicit or explicit principles, norms, rules and decision-making procedures around which actors' expectations converge in a given area of international relations".[8] Thus, regimes are the mediums through which parties can rationally predict the behavior of other parties. In this way, regimes channel the relations of states and promote common frames of reference that may allow cooperation to develop under certain conditions.

It is generally held that regimes must confront one of three conditions to undergo a process of transformation: internal contradiction, shifts in the power structure of the actors, or the impact of exogenous forces. It is worthwhile keeping this in mind when one considers the Nile Water regime over the course of time.

---

[6] Ibid.
[7] Ibid, pp. 103, 101.
[8] Stephen Krasner, "Structural Causes and Regime Consequences" in Stephen Krasner, ed. *International Regimes* (Ithaca and London: Cornell University Press, 1983) p. 2.

The Nile river regime is a security regime. The distinctiveness of security regimes stems from the phenomenon known as the "security dilemma", which makes security regimes "especially valuable and especially difficult to achieve".[9] The "security dilemma" phenomenon is a situation in which a state working to maintain its security is regarded by others as threatening their own security, thus triggering off actions that the first side would consider infringing on its security, and consequently exacerbating relations between the two sides, i.e., a zero-sum situation. The most important function of a regime, whether a security or a non-security one, is to converge expectations in a particular issue area. It clarifies "what states are (not) permitted to do in a given issue-area",[10] and thus restrains the actions of the regime's members.

The strength of a security regime depends on the degree of institutionalization of the regime. However, informal regimes might at times be a blessing. "It is precisely the informality of most security regimes, ..., their capacity to build on tacit consensus, to exploit common aversions which are mutually shared, which gives them special potential in an environment that is coldly inhospitable to more formal arrangements".[11] Nonetheless, the lack of institutions has a negative effect in the long-term, as institutions help to increase the cost of defection. Institutions also help to cement relations among the members of the regime and create common identity.[12]

The Nile regime lacks an institutional framework. No supra-national authority has been established to take over planning for the river, nor does a multilateral treaty govern relations among all riparian polities. This has affected the regime: it has been, and is, a loose regime that depends mainly on the presence of a hegemonic power. As long as a hegemon has existed and the regime addressed the minimum needs of the actors involved (that is,

---

[9] Robert Jervis, "Security Regimes" in Stephen ed., p. 174.
[10] Volker Rittberger, Manfred Efinger, and Martin Mender, "Toward an East-West Security Regime: The Case of Confidence- and Security-Building Measures", *Journal of Peace and Research*, 27, no. 1: 55-74, 1990, p. 57.
[11] Janice Gross Stein, "Detection and Defection: Security 'Regimes' and the Management of International Conflict", *International Conflict*, 40: 599-627, Autumm 1985, p. 624.
[12] Neta Crawford, "A Security Regime Among Democracies: Cooperation Among Iroquois Nationa", *International Organization*, 48: 345-85, Summer 1994, pp. 376-79, 380.

the demands of the parties to the regime remained relatively low), the regime has functioned well. However, there are already indications that demands are growing higher. Thus, with the lack of institutions to cushion the negative effect of the rising stakes, the existing regime can be expected to suffer.

In principle, regional regimes are similar to global ones in terms of their construction, maintenance and transformation. In that respect, regional hegemons undertake all efforts needed to construct and maintain the regional system that serves their interests. However, regional hegemons are different from the global ones in that they must take into consideration the global powers as they construct and maintain regional regimes. Thus, their ability to construct and maintain regimes are more limited.

The Nile regime was developed initially under the influence of Britain, which was both a regional hegemon and a global superpower. However, once Egypt maintained the regime as a regional hegemon, after the mid-1950s, it had to consider the position of superpowers in the area. Egypt employed the opportunity offered by its geostrategic position offered to enhance its connections with superpowers. However, Egyptian attempts to maintain the regime have also suffered from superpower intervention, for example in the aid given to Ethiopia by the United States during the 1950s and by the Soviet Union in the 1970s and 1980s for Nile-related studies. The contemporary story of Nilopolitics is very much the story of Egypt's role as a hegemon.

CHAPTER ONE

EGYPT'S IMPERIAL ATTEMPT

Until the 1870s, Britain was the strongest European power with an interest in the African continent in general, and East Africa in particular. British interests were rooted in the area's location relative to Britain's Indian and South African possessions. Nonetheless, London long refrained from establishing an African Empire. Instead, the British worked with local African powers to ensure free trade while avoiding the expense of direct rule. France and Portugal also utilized existing African political entities to protect their interests. In the West, it was the Kingdom of Congo with whom Portugal had excellent relations. In the North it was the Bey of Tunisia and the Khedive of Egypt whom France and Britain utilized. As for the East, the Sultan of Zanzibar was the major actor.[1]

African Players

In the absence of direct rule by a European state,[2] the native African polities pursued their own interests. Three notable polities were dominant along the Nile valley; Egypt, Abyssinia and Buganda. Egypt was by far the most modernized and powerful of the three. It enjoyed a well-established nationhood, dating back many centuries, as well as a particularly strong central government. In the early nineteenth century, under its modernizing leader Mohamed Ali, Egypt also enjoyed a technological edgeover other African polities. This allowed it to project power beyond its borders. Modern weapons and means of transportation allowed Egyptian rulers to extend their domain up the Nile Valley, conquering less advanced and politically weaker African polities. The most comprehensive attempt toward this goal was the construction of the Egyptian Equatorial African Empire

---

[1] Robert O. Collins, *European in Africa* (New York: Alfred A. Knopf, 1971) pp. 358-9.

[2] European powers did interfere at times when their interests required intervention such as the British campaign against Abyssinia in 1867 and again when Britain intervened in the dispute between Egypt and Zanzibar over possessions in the East African coast in favour of the Sultan of Zanzibar in 1875-6.

during the reign of Khedive Ismail of Egypt 1863-1879). Although Egypt extended its sovereignty over the equatorial lakes, the attempt failed to conquer the two other strong African polities that existed along the Nile valley; the Kingdom of Abyssinia along the Blue Nile and the Kingdom of Buganda along the Equatorial Lakes.

Khedive Ismail's effort to create an Egyptian empire on the Nile was partly motivated by a hydraulic imperative: to secure the sources of the Nile. Other factors--economic interests and the temptation created by a local balance of power that clearly favored Egypt--cannot be overlooked. But the security of the Nile's sources was also a factor. When Ismail learned that an Italian expedition was to be sent to the Sobat river and other sources of the Nile, he instructed the Governor-General of Egypt's equatorial province to proceed to the Sobat and claim it for Egypt. Ismail asserted that no European power must be admitted to the sources of the Nile.[3] A similar position was taken by Ismail in reaction to the Stanley campaign in Uganda, which he viewed as a British encroachment on the other source of the Nile.[4]

Egypt's efforts to expand along the Nile agreed, in part, with British policies in Africa. However, the role played by Britain in the search for an Egyptian Empire in Africa was minimal, and often obstructive. Relations between Egypt and Britain were complex at the time. Britain had high stakes in Egypt that included the Egyptian shares in the Suez Canal company that Britain bought as well as a high level of commerce. In fact, by 1890, almost 80 per cent of Egyptian exports went to Britain while Egypt received about half of its imports from this country.[5] Moreover, although Egypt was nominally under Turkish suzerainty, it was the subject of foreign intervention, especially with the formation in 1876 of the *caisse de la dette* which included Britain, France and Germany and had jurisdiction over Egyptian finances. Although Egypt historically oscillated between a global pro-French and pro-British policy, by the time of Khedive Ismail,

---

[3] Letter of Khedive Ismail to Gordon, Abdin files 71/4 translated and quoted in George Guindi, *Ismail* (Cairo: Matba`at dar al-Kutub al-Masraiah, 1947) pp. 255-6.
[4] Conversation between Khedive Ismail and Chaille-Long translated and quoted in Guindi, p. 256
[5] Robert O. Collins, *The Waters of The Nile: Hydropolitics and the Jongli Canal 1900-1988* (Oxford: Clarendon Press, 1990) p. 30.

Egypt was closer to Britain. That was more true as France opposed many of the reforms championed by Ismail, like judicial reform and changing the Suez Canal Company charter.[6]

Thus, Egypt, at the accession of Ismail in 1863, was considered a British ally. Egypt extended logistical support to Britain twice: when the latter needed to move its troops to face the Indian mutiny of 1857 and when it needed to launch a punitive expedition against Ethiopia in 1867.[7] Khedive Ismail recognized this relation and wished to mobilize British help in his schemes. He positioned Egypt's attempts to expand in Africa in accordance with Britain's declared policies of fighting the slave trade and expanding legitimate commerce in central Africa. This was one of the reasons why Ismail appointed two British citizens, Sir Samuel Baker and Charles Gordon, to command Egypt's conquests in central Africa.[8] Both men were also appointed for their knowledge of the area. However, this did not imply an official British role in Egypt's conquests. Thus, the British government insisted that no assistance could be provided to Baker.[9] Moreover, Britain opposed Egypt's expansion in the Red Sea littoral and supported Zanzibar in its conflict with Egypt over possessions in East Africa: London exerted pressure on Egypt to withdraw.[10] Moreover, Egyptian fear of British intentions along the Nile river can be seen from Khedive Ismail's message to the American Lieutenant-Colonel Charles Chaille-Long, General Gordon's chief-of-staff, ordering him to reach Uganda before the Stanley expedition. Ismail feared that Stanley would claim Uganda for Britain.[11] Fear of British expansionism was also evident in Cairo's suspicion of the British conquest of Abyssinia. In this campaign, Egypt extended help to Britain in order to keep an eye on the British and make sure they would leave as soon as they accomplished their objectives.[12] Finally, the British nationality of Egypt's commanders in central Africa does not, by itself,

---

[6] M. F. Shukry, *The Khedive Ismail and Slavery in the Sudan 1863-1879* (Cairo: Librairie la Resistance, 1938) p. 28.
[7] Ibid, p. 31.
[8] John Flint, "The Wider Background to Partition and Colonial Occupation" in Roland Oliver and Gervase Mathew, eds., *History of East Africa*, Vol. 1 (Oxford: Claredon Press, 1963) p. 358.
[9] Shukry, pp. 157, 158, 179.
[10] Flint, p. 38.
[11] Quoted in Guindi, p. 256.
[12] Shukry, pp. 246-7.

indicate an alliance between Britain and Egypt with regard to the Egyptian African Empire. At the time, the Egyptian army had officers from many European countries as well as American ones. Indeed, the head of the Egyptian army during the first Abyssinian campaign was a Swiss, Werner Munzinger, who had previously worked as the French councilor in the area.[13] Egypt's attempt to construct an Empire along the Nile valley was mainly an Egyptian effort, rooted in the recognition of the importance of the Nile water to Egypt. However, Egypt's pursuit of its national interests agreed with European interest in Africa.[14]

The other African polity that had long existed was Abyssinia (also known as Ethiopia). However, unlike Egypt, Abyssinia suffered from a long period of disintegration and the failure of its central government to hold the country together. The latest of these periods began in the late 17th century and continued until the reign of King Theodore II, who restored Abyssinian unity in 1855 and adopted the title of Emperor of all Ethiopia. There ensued a period of relative stability and the building of a strong centralized state. However, Ethiopia soon ran into trouble with the European powers in 1864 when it detained a number of European citizens, including some British diplomats.[15] This set off a British campaign to release the prisoners and ended in the full occupation of the Abyssinian capital and the suicide of King Theodore II.[16] Nevertheless, the British forces soon withdrew and the central government was restored by King John, a very ambitious monarch who attempted to extend his reign throughout East Africa. However, his attempts soon conflicted with the Egyptian Empire in East Africa and later with both the Italians and the Mahdist forces of the Sudan. King John was killed by a "chance bullet" and his forces were routed by the Sudanese in 1889.[17] After a brief period of civil unrest, King Menelik became the Emperor of all Ethiopia.

The third African polity of major importance was Buganda, which by the 19th century was in control of the northeastern area off Lake Victoria, or

---

[13] Ibid, pp. 242, 249.
[14] Haggai Erlich, *Ethiopia and the Middle East* (Boulder, Lynne Rienner Publishers, 1994) p. 55.
[15] Shukry, p. 245.
[16] Eduard Fueter, *World History 1815-1920* (New York: Harcourt, Brace and Company, 1922) p. 342.
[17] Collins, *European in Africa*, p. 73.

the southern part of today's Uganda.[18] This kingdom was rising at the expense of an older feudal kingdom, Bunyoro. Unlike Bunyoro, Buganda had a strong central government.[19] This government was able to build a strong army[20] as well as achieve advances in the fields of agriculture and construction. Indeed, the land of Buganda was very rich and the amount of rainfall enabled the country to develop year-round agriculture. The country's main trading partner was Zanzibar, which was the most active trading polity on the African east coast. Through this trade, the Kingdom of Buganda was able to acquire modern rifles that represented the main weapons of the elite Bugandan forces, although most troops were still armed with spears. Nonetheless, rifle-power and the ability of the central government to mobilize its power enabled Buganda to extend its domain and to defeat its traditional rival, Bunyoro.[21] However, by extending its domain outward, Buganda came in contact with Egypt, which was attempting to extend its domain southward towards the sources of the Nile.

Relations among the three African polities mentioned above were fundamentally bilateral and highly competitive. Egypt and Ethiopia had a long history of relations that varied from cooperation to conflict. With the reemergence of the Kingdom of Ethiopia under King Theodore II in 1855, relations between the two African polities were strained. On one level, Ethiopia stressed its traditional Christian identity. Thus, it considered its encirclement by Muslim-held territories--what was called "the encroachments of the Turks and Egyptians"--as threatening.[22] Ethiopia's major interest in expanding its territory was to have a port on the Red Sea, which Egypt was aggressively consolidating under its domain during the reign of Khedive Ismail.[23] For its part, Egypt was attempting to place the whole of the Nile basin under its domain. In addition to the Sudan, the Egyptian Empire extended to the East African coast of the Red Sea in what was known as the

---

[18] For other African polities on the Equatorial Lakes, please refer to Oliver, pp. 169-211 and Low, pp. 297-351.
[19] Roland Oliver, "Discernible Developments in the Interior c. 1500-1840" in Roland Oliver and Gervase Mathew eds., p. 189.
[20] Ibid, p. 190.
[21] D.A. Low, "The Northern Interior, 1840-84" in Roland Oliver and Gervase Mathew eds., pp. 332, 334-35.
[22] Shukry, pp. 245, 257.
[23] For Egyptian expansion in the East African coast, and the Red Sea littoral, see Shukry, 1938 pp. 238-72.

Eastern Sudan province. Moreover, Egypt in its attempts to dominate the Central African Plateau of the Nile Valley planned to establish a network of garrison stations from the coast to the inland areas.[24] Thus, relations between Ismail and the different Ethiopian Kings were strained. Open war started between Egypt and Ethiopia in 1875. Many Egyptian campaigns were dispatched to Ethiopia in 1875 and 1876, but all failed to defeat the armies of King John. Instead, the Egyptian army suffered a major defeat at the battle of Kaya Khor in 1876 near the city of Gura.[25] However, the Egyptians regrouped in Gura and were able to deny the Ethiopians the fruits of their victory by defeating the advancing Ethiopian army. King John's offer to end the war between the two countries was accepted. Ethiopia retreated to Aduwa while the Egyptians retired to Massawa on the coast. This ended Egyptian attempts to invade Ethiopia. However, Egypt was able to consolidate its empire on the African coast of the Red Sea, in Eastern Sudan and in Somaliland.[26]

Egyptian relations with Buganda were much different. Egypt's attempts to take over the Kingdom of Buganda were less militaristic and more diplomatic. After reaching the Equatorial lakes area in 1874 to assert Egyptian sovereignty over the area, the British commander of the Egyptian army, General Gordon realized that the strongest kingdom in the area was Buganda. He tried to convince the Kabaka (King) of Buganda to place himself under the protection of the Khedive while maintaining his rule. The Kabaka was interested only in having an equal treaty of alliance between Egypt and Buganda.[27] The Kabaka's main goal was to defeat his traditional enemy, the Bunyoro. However, Gordon's resources were very limited and he had no wish to get involved in local disputes. Thus, he declined the Kabaka's request for military support. The first Egyptian mission in 1874 was very successful in establishing the foundation of bilateral relations between Egypt and Buganda. However, frictions later developed and resulted in the detention of an Egyptian garrison in Buganda. This threatened to start a war but the crisis was defused and the Egyptian forces were allowed to withdraw from Bugandan territories.[28] Thus, while Egypt was able to

---

[24] Flint, pp. 358-59.
[25] Shukry, pp. 258-59, 268-69.
[26] Ibid, pp. 269-70.
[27] Low, p. 341.
[28] Low, pp. 341-42.

construct an empire that included most of the Nile valley, it was unable to break down the Bugandan and the Ethiopian resistance.

Instead of trying to build a regime to accommodate the needs of other African polities, Egypt relied on military force to try to extend its rule over the sources of the Nile. This was evident in the contract between the Egyptian government and Sir Samuel Baker, whom Khedive Ismail entrusted to conquer the equatorial province. The contract described the primary objective of Sir Samuel's service as being "to annex all the countries that comprises the Nile basin in Central Africa".[29] With regard to Ethiopia, it recognized the strong position that country enjoyed vis-a-vis Egypt with regard to the Nile waters. In its dispute with Egypt, and in its attempt to become a major power in the area, Ethiopia threatened to cut off Egypt's water supply. In the words of King Theodore of Ethiopia, he wished to divert "the water of the Nile into another channel and thus to ruin or subdue Egypt".[30] However, he did not have the ability to do this. As for Buganda, no evidence remains of its strategic thought. Perhaps, its leaders did not recognize the strategic leverage they had on Egypt. However, they certainly resisted Egyptian infringement on their territories and repeatedly opposed Egyptian attempts to plant a garrison on the shores of Lake Victoria.

No regime existed to regulate international relations among riparian polities when the Egyptian Empire in Africa declined in the 1880s. Egypt was unable to act as a hegemon in the Nile valley in a way to enable it to construct a regime. As a hegemon, Egypt would have been expected to provide public goods, in that case, stability and military assistance. In Buganda, General Gordon declined to assist Buganda when it requested Egyptian help in its war with Bunyoro. With the arrival of Sir Henry Morton Stanley to Buganda and his willingness to assist this country in its fight, Egypt lost a bargaining card and Buganda was more inclined to be independent-minded.[31] As for Ethiopia, instead of supporting that country in its dispute with Britain, Egypt had provided assistance to the latter.[32] Nevertheless, all the territories not under direct Egyptian rule, were under

---

[29] Abdin Correspondence 72/1 quoted in Shukry, Appendix A; Guindi, 1947: 235.
[30] Quoted in Shukry, p. 259.
[31] Low, p. 341.
[32] Shukry, pp. 246-7.

the rule of technologically backward African kingdoms incapable of threatening Egypt's interests in the Nile water.[33] Indeed, the simple interests of Ethiopia and Buganda did not require much utilization of the Nile water. Thus, despite the absence of a clear regime along the Nile valley, Egypt was not truly challenged by any power that affected its access to the water of the Nile. This continued to be true until the European powers began interfering more directly in the African continent.

European Control of Africa

The nature of European intersts in Africa changed after 1870. This was due to two fundamental reasons. First, the opening of the Suez canal in 1869 altered the political map of Africa, creating new centers of interest and changing the European relationship with the African continent in general and East Africa in particular. East Africa now was about 6000 miles closer to Europe. It was also on the major and shortest route to India.[34] Thus, a new importance evolved for East Africa, whether for the British who were trying to ensure the consolidation of their empire,[35] or for other European powers challenging the *status quo*. New places, such as Aden and Zanzibar, gained special importance. This important geographical/political development also coincided with a medical development that facilitated the European conquest of Africa: the discovery of quinines. Another technological development that figured in Europe's intervention in Africa was the development of the steamship.[36]

However, the main impetus for Europe's presence in the African continent was due to the changing European balance of power. Germany's victory over France in 1870 made Germany the strongest continental power. However, this was not sufficient for Germany and it soon began to challenge the British hegemony over the seas by launching a strong fleet of its own. On the other hand, France lost its European standing following the

---

[33] Thomas Naff and Ruth Matson eds.,*Water in the Middle East: Conflict or Cooperation* (Boulder: Westview Press, 1984) p. 141.
[34] W.E.F. Ward, W.E.F. and L.W. White, *East Africa: A Century of Change 1870-1970* (New York: Africana Publishing Corportaion, 1972) p. 9.
[35] Sir John Gray, "Zanzibar and the Coastal Belt 1840-84" in Roland Oliver and Gervase Mathew eds., p. 242.
[36] Collins, *European in Africa*, pp. 69-70.

Franco-Prussian war of 1870. This induced France to search for a new dimension to assert national power and prestige. Thus, France extended its existing empire and projected French power into new places in Africa.[37] In addition, medium-sized powers began to challenge the global standing of the great European powers. Italy, though less powerful than Germany, was also assertive when it came to the establishment of an empire. Belgium also began to assert itself in the field of empire-building.

The prelude to Europe's scramble for Africa was the British occupation of Egypt. The occupation was affected without undue difficulty. In one afternoon, the Egyptian army was routed in el-Tel el-Kabir.[38] In occupying Egypt, Britain declared that its intentions were not imperial. On the contrary, Britain declared its purpose to be that of restoring the rule of the Khedive and bringing Egypt's finances into order. It estimated the time required for this job to fall somewhere between two months and two years. However, the British occupation of Egypt antagonized France.[39] France considered Egypt as a country in which it enjoyed a special status.[40] Moreover, France considered that Britain had cheated her out of Egypt,[41] as the invitation to bomb Alexandria which France declined to participate in did not originally include the occupation of Egypt. Furthermore, France was one of Egypt's largest trade partners and had a major interest in the Suez Canal.[42] A unilateral British action in Egypt threatened to endanger French interests. Britain tried to assure France that its status in Egypt was only interim and worked to preserve French interests in the country. However, this did not stop France as well as other European countries from regarding the British suspiciously.

In 1884, Germany and France called for a congress to discuss colonial matters in Africa.[43] The 1884 Congress of Berlin was the prelude to the European division of Africa. This had a profound effect on the establishment of a regime on the Nile.

---

[37] Ibid, pp. 67-68.
[38] Collins, *European in Africa*, p. 72.
[39] Flint, p. 363.
[40] Collins, *The Waters of the Nile*, p. 33.
[41] Ward and White, p. 28.
[42] Collins, *The Waters of the Nile*, p. 34.
[43] Ward and White, p. 30; Collins, *European in Africa*, p. 77.

CHAPTER TWO

BRITAIN: THE MASTER OF THE NILE

The balance of power in Africa among the European powers in the late nineteenth century reflected the balance of power in Europe. By the mid-1870s, two blocks of countries developed out of the existing great powers: the Triple alliance and the Dual alliance. Between the two blocks, Britain acted as a balancer, attempting to maintain the *status quo*.

Great Britain primarily sought to maintain the *status quo* among European powers and to thwart an overall European war. A major concern of Britain in pursuing its relations with other European powers was to preserve its Indian empire. Thus, Britain was worried about any disruption of its strategic routes to India.[1] Britain followed a grand strategy of controlling choke points. As a predominantly naval power, the control of possible choke points along known maritime routes was the supreme British interest. This led to British efforts to control South Africa, Gibraltar, Aden, Singapore and the Suez Canal.

Colonial Interests

Direct British involvement in East Africa can be traced to the occupation of Egypt in 1882. Only twice before had Britain interfered directly in the area; once when British diplomats were held by the King of Ethiopia and a second time when Egypt and Zanzibar had a dispute over territories on the Red Sea coast. However, on those two occasions, British interventions were brief. British troops evacuated Ethiopia after the hostages were released and the Ethiopian King slain, while in the second incident political rather than military pressure was used to force Egypt out of the disputed territories.[2] Even the occupation of Egypt was initially intended to be of a short duration. Why, then, did the occupation last for more than 70 years?

---

[1] Patricia Wright, *Conflict on the Nile: The Fashoda Incident of 1898* (London: Heinemann, 1972) p. 9.
[2] Flint, p. 359; Shukry, p. 245.

The most plausible explanation is Egypt's strategic importance to British global interests. The Suez canal was of major importance. The logic of the British policy was that if some European power had to interfere in Egypt, it would best be Great Britain.[3]

However, having decided to remain in Egypt, Britain realized that the security of Egypt had to be gained elsewhere. Indeed, Egypt's absolute security lay in securing the water of the Nile, without which the country would turn into a desert. As long as Britain regarded its presence in Egypt as temporary, it did not care much about the colonization of East Africa. However, once the British presence was taken as long-lasting, London could not remain indifferent to who ruled the sources of the Nile. This took the British deep into Central and Eastern Africa.[4]

The three immediate places that posed a threat to Egyptian interests in the Nile were the Sudan, Ethiopia and Uganda. The Sudan was, for the time, under the rule of the Mahdi[5] and his followers and had no means to block the Nile water. Limiting the possibility of a threat from only Ethiopia and Uganda, Britain chose to concentrate its efforts on Uganda as the geographic belief of the time was that Egypt received most of the Nile water from the tropical lakes rather than the Ethiopian plateau. This explains the British decision regarding the colonization of East Africa, the area that now includes Kenya and Uganda.[6] Later, however, Britain decided to reconquer the Sudan because of what it considered the dangerous claims of other European powers to territories near the sources of the Nile.

The second power of relevance to the Nile was Germany. Germany did not have any deep-rooted interests in the Nile. Indeed, for a long time Germany did not have any deep interest in colonies *per se*, as can be seen from its repeated refusal to establish colonies in the 1870s and early 1880s in different parts of the world, including East Africa.[7] However, it was the aim of German policy to prevent any unfriendly alliance among European powers, and especially between Britain and France. One method of doing so

---

[3] Ward and White, p. 28.
[4] Ward and White, p. 37; Collins, *European in Africa*, pp. 79-80; Collins, *The Waters of the Nile*, p. 36.
[5] The Mahdi, an Arabic word meaning Messiah, was the religious and political leader of the Sudanese, during their revolt against Turco-Egyptian rule in 1880s.
[6] Collins, *The Waters of the Nile*, p. 38; Flint, p. 380.
[7] Fueter, pp. 326-27; Flint, pp. 364-65.

was by driving a wedge between the two countries over colonial issues. Thus, Germany encouraged Britain to take control over Egypt, a country France considered within its own sphere of influence.[8] Germany also tried to ensure British dependency on German help regarding many issues, such as, for example, those before the *caisse de la dette* on which Germany sat.[9] Eventually, Germany sought to establish colonies adjacent to important British and French ones. Germany used those colonies to obtain concessions from other powers, Britain included, in Europe, which was the primary target of German foreign policy. Accordingly, Germany chose with care the places it attempted to colonize in East Africa. They were located along the British sea-route to India, i.e. in the German East-Africa colony, as well as in Uganda, where one source of the Nile originates. The latter helped make the position of Britain in Egypt more dependent on German cooperation.

A third country that had profound interests in the Nile was France. France considered Egypt to be within its sphere of influence. It also felt that Britain had cheated it out of the country through its unilateral invasion. French strategists came up with the idea that through controlling the sources of the Nile, France would be able to drive Britain out of Egypt, and solve what came to be known as the "Egyptian question" in its favour. This intention became clear in a lecture given at the *Institute d'Egypte* in Paris, entitled *"Soudan Nilotique"*, by the French hydrologist Victor Prompt in 1893. In his lecture, Prompt explained that any power controlling the area where the White Nile meets the Sobat river would dominate the destiny of Egypt. His argument was that by building a dam to block the Nile water in the Fashoda area, France would be able to control the flow of water and master the destiny of Egypt either by turning the country into a barren desert or by flooding it.[10] That reasoning, as is now known, was both simplistic and faulty. First, the belief that most of the water reaching Egypt came from the White Nile was not accurate.[11] In fact about 85% of the water coming to Aswan originates in the Ethiopian plateau.[12] In addition, the possibility of

---

[8] Collins, *The Waters of the Nile*, pp. 33-34.
[9] Wright, p. 30.
[10] Collins, *The Waters of the Nile*, pp. 49-50; Wright, p. 45; Collins, *European in Africa*, p. 83.
[11] Collins, *European in Africa*, p. 38.
[12] John Waterbury, *Hydropolitics of the Nile Valley* (Syracuse: Syracuse University Press, 1979) p. 23.

building a dam where the White Nile meets the Sobat or, in other terms, Fashoda, was at least technically doubtful. However, the lecture came at a time when these geographic and topographic facts were unknown.[13]

Italian interests in East Africa were in many aspects similar to those of France. Italy joined the ranks of great European powers late in the century and lacked the great military power that could be mustered by Germany, its fellow late comer. It aimed to establish its prestige and achieve an equal footing with its neighboring European countries. Italy's method in doing so was to establish an empire.[14] Short of financial resources, and lacking a global fleet, Italy chose Africa. Outmaneuvered by France in Tunisia, Italy directed its attention mainly to East Africa. This was the nearest territory not claimed by any European powers and not threatening the interests of any other power. The Italian colonies were also to be used to ease the overpopulation problem by providing opportunities to immigrants who in time would channel back economic benefits to their home country.[15]

Outside East Africa, but with strategic importance to the area, was the Belgian Congo, or what was known as the Congo Free State. Belgian interests in the Congo were minimal.[16] The colony was actually the private property of King Leopold II and frequently the government of Belgium was unaware of his actions in Africa.[17] However, regardless of the decision making process, King Leopold II was the ruler of both territories and was therefore able to use Belgium's resources and relations with other European powers to help his schemes in Africa. Belgian-British relations were good in Europe. Moreover, despite an initial preference for Portuguese sovereignty over the Congo, Britain helped the Congo Free State to expand in central Africa.[18]

Britain had a genuine interest in the waters of the Nile because of its geostrategic interest in Egypt. Britain was also the most influential power in East Africa. In addition to its strong navy, which was not yet challenged in the Red Sea, Britain had a direct military presence in both Aden and Egypt, as well as Zanzibar, which was a British client. Further increasing

---

[13] Flint, p. 366.
[14] Collins, *The Waters of the Nile*, p. 55.
[15] Fueter, p. 326.
[16] Collins, *European in Africa*, p. 73.
[17] Collins, *The Waters of the Nile*, p. 54; Flint, p. 362.
[18] Wright, p. 49.

British power in the area was the large human and material resources available for use in Africa. All the other powers suffered from lack of required funds, material and human resources, and/or military might that could be devoted to colonial projects in East Africa. The only country that had all the requirements was Germany. However, that country was more interested in Europe than in Africa and preferred to work in concert rather than in conflict with Britain. Thus, Britain had all the requirements of a hegemon interested in, and capable of, building an international regime to serve its interests.

The British-Built Regime

The international regime built by the British on the Nile aimed to ensure the priority of Egyptian needs in the utilization of Nile waters. One purpose of the regime was to prevent the seizure of the Nile's upper sources by unfriendly powers. Other than Britain, the European powers operating in East Africa during the last two decades of the century, namely Germany, Italy, Belgium's Congo Free State and France were interested parties. In addition, Ethiopia, the only African polity in East Africa that had maintained its independence, was also involved. In this aspect of the regime, the benefits (or "common goods") provided by the hegemonic power were (1) the peaceful distribution of African colonies and (2) helping other European powers to consolidate their spheres of influence.

Britain maintained the Nile regime in three different ways. First, it used diplomatic and political power to exclude potential adversaries from the Nile basin, while compensating them elsewhere in Africa and Europe. This method was used particularly with Germany. The second way Britain maintained the regime was by allowing what it considered friendly powers, or at least weak powers, to approach the sources of the Nile. However, Britain made sure to restrict these powers through international treaties that would limit their freedom of action with regards to the waters of the Nile. This method was used with Italy, the Belgian Congo-Free State and Ethiopia. The third method was used only when Britain feared the collapse of the whole regime and when it was confronted with a power that might compromise the whole regime. In such a case, Britain used military force to drive a threatening power away from the Nile valley. This was mainly used with France during the Fashoda incident. As for the Sudan, which was under the control of the technologically-backward Mahdi regime, Britain was happy see the Sudan serving as a geographic buffer. However, when a French invasion of the upper sources of the Nile appeared possible, Britain used military force to reconquer the Sudan. Through these three ways, Britain was able to maintain its regime.

Using Diplomacy to Exclude Potential Adversaries. The German claim for a colony in East Africa presented a challenge to Britain. On one level, because of global considerations, Britain was forced to cooperate with Germany, and indeed to call on German help regarding many issues. On the other hand, the territories claimed by Germany were claimed by the Sultan of Zanzibar, who was not only a British client but also an important instrument of British policy in the area. Britain gave priority to its global considerations and allowed Germany to establish a colony in what became later German East Africa.[19] The British government declared that "Her Majesty's Government are favourable to German enterprise in districts not occupied by any civilized power".[20] Abandoned by his allies, the Sultan of Zanzibar was forced to yield to German demands and accept German sovereignty over parts of Eastern Africa as well as usage of the Port of Dar-es-Salaam. Britain and Germany then proceeded to delimit the possessions of the Sultan.[21] The Sultan was soon to lose all his mainland possessions and be limited to the island of Zanzibar.

The 1890 Anglo-German treaty came in a wider context of sorting out the global relations of the two countries and preempting future conflict. According to the agreement Britain helped the Germans consolidate their possessions in Tanganyika by exerting pressure on Zanzibar's Sultan to cede some territories and not to obstruct German efforts in the area. In addition, Britain "played its trump card"; the ceding of the Heligoland island to Germany. The island was of major strategic importance to Germany as it blocked the free naval exit of the German navy to the North Sea. The price was high and domestic opposition by the cabinet and the Queen had to be overcome before the British Prime Minister was able to extend his offer to

---

[19] Flint, pp. 369, 370-71.
[20] F.O. 84/1722 on 20 May 1885 quoted in Flint, p. 371.
[21] Ward and White, p. 34.

Germany.[22] Germany accepted, clearly valuing the long-term interest in Europe over a possible interest in a far away colony in East Africa.[23] In return, Britain received German recognition of its protectorate over Zanzibar and the Pempa islands, the recognition that Uganda fell within the British sphere of interests (thus securing the free flow of the Nile water from Lake Victoria to Egypt) and the dropping of German claims for territories north of the Anglo-German agreement of 1886 delimiting the British and German sphere of influence in East Africa (thus eliminating German pockets north of the border).[24] "The effect of this agreement", wrote the British Prime Minister Lord Salisbury to the British ambassador to Berlin, "will be that, except so far as the Congo State is concerned, there will be no European competitor to British influence between the first degree of South Latitude and the borders of Egypt".[25]

Using Diplomacy to Accommodate "Friendly" Powers. Italy was the other European power that was dangerously near the sources of the Nile. Italy and Britain enjoyed good relations at the time of the Africa rush. However, when Italy signed the treaty of Ucciali with Ethiopia, which according to Italy effectively recognized it as the protector of Ethiopia, alarm bells started ringing in London and Cairo.[26] The source of unease was the ancient Ethiopian claim to the sources of the Blue Nile. This was exacerbated by the Italian claim to Kassala, previously, an Egyptian possession that had been evacuated during the Mahdi rebellion. Control of Kassala would have given Italy command of the sources of the River Atbara, one of the sources of the Nile. Britain started negotiating with Italy, with the specific objective of "insist[ing] on the command of all the affluents of the Nile, so far as Egypt formerly possessed them".[27]

Negotiations between the two parties led Britain to recognize the Italian protectorate of Ethiopia in 1891. However, the borders of Ethiopia were drawn so as to maintain the whole of the Blue Nile beyond Italian control.[28]

---

[22] Flint, pp. 383, 384.
[23] Ward and White, p. 43.
[24] Ibid, pp. 42-43.
[25] Quoted in Collins, *The Waters of the Nile*, p. 48.
[26] Flint, p. 385.
[27] Salisbury to Baring, 31 Aug. 1890 quoted in Flint, p. 385
[28] Flint, p. 385.

Regarding Kassala, Britain agreed to allow an Italian presence in the area as a military need, in return for Italian recognition of Kassala as belonging to Egypt, to which it would be restored when Egyptian rule returned to the Sudan (which took place in 1897).[29] The 1891 agreement stipulated that "The Government of Italy undertakes not to construct on the Atbara any irrigation or other works that might sensibly modify its flow into the Nile".[30] Thus, while allowing Italy to colonize Ethiopia, Britain guaranteed Egypt's interests by securing the uninterrupted flow of Nile water.

Italy's colonial project in Ethiopia failed to materialize. Following the consolidation of the rule of King Menelik II, a rift developed between the Ethiopian Kingdom and Italy. This culminated in a war that ended with an Ethiopian triumph at the battle of Aduwa in 1896.[31] Italy's presence on the banks of the Nile was temporarily ended. With Ethiopia now controlling the sources of the Blue Nile, as well as claiming its western borders to be the eastern banks of the White Nile, Britain faced a new challenge to the Egyptian interests in the Nile.[32]

While Ethiopia's technological backwardness rendered it incapable of threatening the waters of the Nile on its own, it nevertheless represented a potential threat because of its ties to other European powers. The most important of these were the Russians and the French, both of which were hostile to Britain.[33] Britain futilely attempted to convince Ethiopia to drop its claim to the eastern banks of the White Nile. The problem was solved by the Anglo-Egyptian reconquest of the Sudan in 1898, which left both banks of the White Nile in their hands. Anglo-Egyptian gunboats were deployed to check Ethiopian claims over the east bank of the White Nile.[34] In 1902, Ethiopia concluded a final agreement with Britain recognizing the borders of the Sudan. Britain also received a concession related to Ethiopia's control over the sources of the Blue Nile. The agreement pledged Ethiopia would

---

[29] Wright, p. 64.
[30] Quoted in Odidi Okidi,"A Review of Treaties on Consumptive Utilization of Waters of Lake Victoria and Nile Drainage Basins" in P. P. Howell and J. A. Allan, eds.,*The Nile:Resources Evaluation, Resources Management, Hydropolitics and Legal Issues* (London: School of Oriental and African Studies - University of London, 1990) p. 197.
[31] Wright, p. 66; Collins, *The Waters of the Nile*, p. 56; Fueter, p. 343.
[32] Collins, *The Waters of the Nile*, p. 56.
[33] Wright, p. 66.
[34] Ibid, pp. 118-19.

"not ... construct or allow to be constructed, any work across the Blue Nile, Lake Tana, or the Sobat which would arrest the flow of their water into the Nile except in agreement with His Britannic Majesty's Government and the Government of the Sudan".[35] In return, Ethiopia received British recognition of its independence. This was the "public good", or at least the reward, provided by Great Britain as hegemon of the Nile regime. This Ethiopian concession was only possible, however, with the humiliating French withdrawal from Fashoda in 1898, which will be discussed below.

Despite its lack of military and political power, the Congo Free State also attempted to intrude on the sources of the Nile. The ruler of the state was extremely ambitious. One of his dreams was to control the sources of the great two rivers of Africa, the Nile and the Congo. He was able to achieve the latter objective. However, holding the sources of the Nile proved to be a more difficult job. King Leopold II sought to extend his sovereignty over Bahr-al-Ghazal province to fill the gap left by the withdrawal of the Egyptian governor of Equatoria, Emin Pasha, who was "rescued" by an expedition sent under the initiative of King Leopold.[36] This preceded the Anglo-Egyptian reconquering of the Sudan, and no European power held legally recognized claims over the area. The only possible claim was that of Egypt. However, it was separated from the province by the Mahdist state in the Sudan and was itself occupied by the British. Moreover, the Anglo-German treaty of 1890 limited the two countries' spheres of influence to their borders with the Congo Free State, thus allowing Leopold to extended his domain to the sources of the Nile, above the territories of Uganda. In the same year he sent an expedition to establish the claim of the Congo Free State through effective occupation. Although expeditions were able to reach the sources of the Nile by 1892, they nevertheless failed to achieve any permanent occupation due to the raids of the Mahdist.[37] Britain acted to defend its interests.

In accordance with the regime described before, the British worked to place the Nile's sources in their own hands or in the hands of friendly powers incapable of challenging British interests. Britain demanded that King Leopold not claim sovereignty over the sources of the Nile. In return,

---

[35] Quoted in Okidi, p. 197
[36] Collins, *The Waters of the Nile*, p. 41.
[37] Ibid, pp. 54.55.

Britain agreed to lease to King Leopold a great area in Bahr-al-Ghazal province, from Lake Albert northward to Fashoda. This had the added benefit of putting the area beyond the reach of France. In exchange, Leopold agreed to cede an area to Britain that would enable it to encircle the German colonies in East Africa and connect British colonies, thus allowing for the possible construction of a Cape-to-Cairo railroad.[38] This deal infuriated both France and Germany, who pressured Leopold to abrogate the treaty.[39] He nevertheless considered as under his control the area leased to him by Britain. He concluded an agreement with France, ceding to the latter all his "leased" area with the exception of a 250 mile strip, known as the "Lado" corridor. This gave France access to the Nile.[40] With the launching of the French Fashoda expedition, and British preparations to confront this expedition, King Leopold attempted to establish his claim to the "Lado Corridor". He sent two expeditions in 1896. However, only one was able to reach the corridor and even that was not able to demonstrate Congolese sovereignty for long, as it had to withdraw shortly.[41] The British were determined not to allow Leopold to control any of the Nile's tributaries and Leopold soon recognized the need to reach a compromise. After the French withdrawal from Fashoda, agreements were concluded in 1908, 1911 and 1912 adjusting borders in central Africa so that territories west of the Nile were restored to the British domain in Uganda in return for adjustments between the Sudan and the Congo. The agreement of 1908 provided that "The Government of the Independent State of Congo undertake not to construct, or allow to be constructed, any work on or near Semiliki or Isango Rivers, which would diminish the volume of water entering Lake Albert, except in agreement with the Sudanese Government".[42]

Using Military Force to Exclude Challengers. Britain's reaction to the French presence near the sources of the Nile was totally different from that of any other European power. The main reason for that was France's outright declaration that it aimed to force the British from

---

[38] Darrell Bates, *The Fashoda Incident of 1898* (Oxford: Oxford University Press, 1984) p. 14.
[39] Wright, p. 50; Bates, p. 16.
[40] Wright, p. 112.
[41] Collins, *The Waters of the Nile*, p. 60; Wright, p. 196; Bates, p. 43.
[42] Quoted in Okidi, p. 198.

Egypt by blocking the flow of the Nile. Following an attempt by the viceroy of Egypt at the time, Khedive `Abbas Hilmi, to follow more independent policies, Britain increased its military presence in Egypt in 1892. As this contradicted the promised British evacuation of Egypt, France demanded that Britain immediately start negotiating its withdrawal. The demand was summarily dismissed.[43] France thereupon prepared an expedition in 1893 to go to Fashoda, which, in addition to being located in the area where all the tributaries of the White Nile meet together to form one big stream, was also the capital of a local African Kingdom, the Shilluk. This added to the political significance of the area as it could have provided France with a legal presence in the area if its protection was recognized by this polity. The logic of France's Fashoda expedition was to force the British to discuss their withdrawal from Egypt, once their stay in Egypt became impossible as a result of French control of the sources of the Nile.[44] However, this expedition failed because of political unrest in France and a lack of cooperation from the Congo-Free State, whose logistical support was essential to the project's success.[45]

The Fashoda project became a central issue within French colonial circles. It was part of the attempt to extend French colonies across Africa, from the Atlantic to Djibouti on the Red Sea. An opportunity presented itself to France with the Italian defeat in Aduwa in 1896, in which the French played a considerable role by supplying Ethiopia with weapons (in violation of the agreement of European powers to abstain from assisting an African polity in a conflict with a European one).[46] Thus, France revived its project to raise the Tricolour on the banks of the Nile. Two expeditions were sent; one through Ethiopia and the other through French possessions in the Congo river basin. The objective of the two missions was to meet in Fashoda. While the expedition from Ethiopia failed to reach its objective, the one from the French Congo reached Fashoda in 1898, hoisted the Tricolour there and signed an agreement with the King of the Shilluk, who recognized French protection of his domain.[47]

---

[43] Collins, *The Waters of the Nile*, pp. 48-49.
[44] Ibid, pp. 49-50; Collins, *European in Africa*, p. 83.
[45] Collins, *European in Africa*, p. 84.
[46] Wright, p. 63-4.
[47] Ibid, pp. 164-65; 169-70. For details of these two expeditions, please refer to Wright.

The British were well aware of French plans. However, they faced a dilemma. Unlike Germany, France had no desire for anything Britain might offer in Europe. Unlike Italy, France already had large possessions in Africa. Britain could not tempt it away from the Nile. Moreover, French intentions were precisely to challenge the regime built by the British on the Nile. Thus, there was no way to accommodate France in the regime. Moreover, a confrontation in Europe was not to the advantage of anyone, and Britain did need France, a major land-power, to contain other growing European powers in the continent, whether the German land-power or to maintain the Ottoman check against the other land-power, Russia. Thus, the confrontation with France had to be limited to Africa, with the least damage to the two countries overall relations.

Three responses were attempted. The first was to send a small force from Uganda, known as the "flying column," down the Nile to occupy Fashoda. However, this effort failed due to the lack of the proper force in Uganda, a rebellion of the Nubians, and delay in the construction of the Uganda railway.[48] The other option was to dissuade Ethiopia and the Congo Free State from assisting the French expeditions, thus making it impossible for them to carry out their mission. However, again, Britain had nothing to offer Ethiopia, especially after they had defeated the Italians and maintained balanced relations with other European powers.[49] On the other hand, the Congo preferred to cooperate with the French.[50] Thus, Britain had to rely on the third option: reconquering the Sudan. The British High Commissioner in Egypt had earlier refused to do this, arguing that the step would entail an expensive and unnecessary campaign because the Mahdist state did not threaten Egyptian interests. The situation changed with the arrival of reports about the French campaign push for Fashoda. Britain could not allow France to threaten its position in Egypt.[51] Thus, an Anglo-Egyptian force in the Sudan met the French expedition in Fashoda in 1898. Militarily, the Anglo-Egyptian force was superior to that of the French. Legally, although France had signed a treaty of protection with the King of the Shilluk, Egypt had the prior right in the area due to its previous occupation. However, the military commanders on the ground agreed to

---

[48] Wright, p. 59; Collins, *The Waters of the Nile*, pp. 58-9; Bates, p. 41-2.
[49] Collins, *The Waters of the Nile*, p. 57; Bates, p. 77.
[50] Wright, pp. 128-29.
[51] Bates, p. 47.

maintain the *status quo* while things were sorted out by politicians in London, Cairo and Paris.[52]

Britain was better placed to achieve its objectives. In military terms, Britain possessed far superior force to that of France in Fashoda, not only in terms of numbers but also armaments and logistics. The French expedition was isolated from other French posts in Djibouti and the French Congo and its supply lines were virtually non-existent. Indeed, the expedition waited for many long months for reinforcements that never came. Moreover, the overall military power of France was inferior to that of Britain. Both in quantitative and qualitative terms, Britain had strengthened its navy with the Royal Navy Act of 1890 that regained the overwhelming British naval superiority.[53]

A bilateral diplomatic solution to the problem was also in Britain's favour. France could not rely on any European power if a European summit was to be held. Germany, which might have supported France to increase the Anglo-French rift in accordance with its long-term policy, was not interested in endangering its growing relations with Britain. Italy, which had recently improved its relations with France after their previous tensions over Tunisia, was also more interested in maintaining good relations with Britain. Even Russia failed to support France in Fashoda.[54] Moreover, Britain did not wish to hold an international conference on the issue and sought to resolve the situation bilaterally with France.

The final element that helped Britain resolve the Fashoda incident in its favor, was the internal disarray into which France had fallen. The incident occurred at the peak of the "Dreyfus Affair" that left France divided and its politicians unable to mobilize the resources of the country in a dispute with Britain. On the other hand, British parties were unified behind the government regarding this issue and demanded the annexation of the whole of the Sudan, including Fashoda.[55] All of the above reasons allowed Britain to prevail and maintain the regime it had constructed along the Nile valley, while forcing France away from the banks of the Nile. In 1904, in what is known as the *entente cordiale*, France dropped all claims to the Nile and recognized the British presence in Egypt. In return, Britain supported French

---

[52] Wright, pp. 169-70. 178.
[53] Ibid, pp. 165, 187-88, 189.
[54] Ibid, p. 188.
[55] Wright, p. 187.

claims in Morocco, the last territory in North Africa not belonging to any specific European sphere of influence.[56]

The other incident in which Britain used military force to maintain its Nile regime was in the Sudan. However, in this case it was not used against the Sudan *per se*. Instead, the Sudan was invaded as a tactical necessity in order to prevent other European powers from controlling the sources of the Nile. Mahdist Sudan was very convenient for the purposes of Britain. Although it controlled virtually all the water that flows into Egypt, the Sudan nevertheless lacked the technological capacity that might have allowed it to threaten this essential resource. Moreover, it was militarily strong enough to ward off any encroachment on the Nile from anything less than forces equipped with modern weapons.[57] However, with the growing interests of other European powers in the area of the White Nile, the necessity of reconquering the Sudan became immediate.[58] The government of Egypt constantly urged the British government to retake the Sudan. Unlike earlier attempts to defeat the Mahdist rebellion, the 1898 campaign was characterized by effective logistical support. The Anglo-Egyptian army defeated the Mahdist forces and occupied their capital, Ommdurman. The Anglo-Egyptian forces then proceeded to confront the French expedition at Fashoda. Possessing superior manpower and firepower, the Anglo-Egyptian army pressed the French to evacuate. This failed, but they nevertheless hoisted the Egyptian flag, claimed sovereignty over the area, and referred the issue to the politicians. The result of the confrontation in Fashoda was the establishment of Anglo-Egyptian sovereignty over the whole of the Sudan.

---

[56] Fueter, p. 337.
[57] Collins, *The Waters of the Nile*, p. 53; Wright, p. 46.
[58] Collins, *The Waters of the Nile*, p. 59.

CHAPTER THREE

BRITAIN THE MODERATOR

By the late nineteenth century, Britain was by far the most important actor on the Nile. This was more true with the marginalization of other European powers along the Nile valley that came at the end of the First World War. As a result of the war, Germany was stripped of its African colonies, which were redistributed among the victorious powers under the mandate system. Though the mandate system aimed at preparing African polities for eventual independence, mandatory powers governed those entities almost like their own colonies. Along the Nile river, the German East Africa colony was divided into three mandated territories, with Urundi and Rwanda going to Belgium while Tanganyika became a British mandate.[1] As for France, it had solved its problems with Britain over colonial matters prior to the First World War in the 1904 agreement that came to be known as the *entente cordiale*. Italy was the only European country present in East Africa that was dissatisfied with its colonies.

Italy had abandoned its allies in the Triple Alliance, Germany and Austria-Hungary, shortly after the start of the war and aligned itself with Britain, France and Russia. In return, Italy expected to be compensated through territorial concessions. It had received an important concession in Europe but felt that it was unfairly compensated in Africa.[2] This was because Britain, France and Belgium were granted the mandates of German African possessions. In consequence, Italy became more determined to build an empire in Africa. In 1935, Italy again invaded Ethiopia. By 1936, it had defeated the African Kingdom and occupied its territories.[3]

---

[1] Kenneth Ingham, "Tanganyika: Slump and Short Term Governors 1932-45" in Vincent Harlow and E.M. Chilver eds., *History of East Africa,* Vol. 2 (Oxford: The Clarendon Press, 1965) p. 543.

[2] Ward and White, p. 91; A. J. Grant and Harold Temperley, *Europe in the Nineteenth and Twentieth Centuries,* 6th ed. (London: Longmans, 1952) pp. 483-84.

The borders of Egypt and the Sudan were adjusted to give more territories to the Italian colony of Libya, including the rich oasis of Kufra, while the border of the British East Africa Protectorate (Kenya) was readjusted to give Italy a new port at Kismayu (Ward & White, p. 91).

[3] Ward and White, pp. 92-93.

The Interwar Period

Although Britain and France opposed the Italian aggression in Ethiopia, they took no action to reverse it. Britain was more interested in preventing another World War. It also needed Italian help to oppose German expansion in Central Europe. On the other hand, France was so worried about the state of affairs in Europe that it was not interested in events in Africa. Germany had already broken two clauses of the treaty of Versailles: the limitations on the size of the German army and its possession of an air force. France worried, quite correctly, that the next step would be the remilitarization of the Rhineland. Italian help to prevent the remilitarization of the Rhineland was more important to France than opposing Italy's actions in Ethiopia.[4]

The British Empire in East Africa did not constitute an integral unit. Instead, each of the colonies was treated as a separate entity, with its own autonomous administration. Thus, in Uganda, local governments were maintained while British officials retained supervisory roles. On the other hand, where there was no tradition of central government, Britain constructed its own administration, as for example in Kenya. In both cases, however, relations with other riparian entities as well as the planning and carrying out of hydraulic projects were purely within the competence of the British administration. Yet, local British administrations worked to serve the limited interests of their respective colonies. The British administration in Egypt was a special case because of the country's long history of central government.

Even before Egypt gained legal independence, a well-established governmental structure was operative in the country. The relative independence of the Egyptian government vis-a-vis the British administration of Egypt increased with time, particularly after the end of the First World War. After a long process of negotiations, Britain granted Egypt legal independence in 1922.

British interests in Egypt remained essentially as described in the previous chapter. However, Britain's position in Egypt was threatened by the nationalist unrest that led to the granting of independence. Britain hoped to avoid any infringement on Egypt's national interests that would rekindle civil disturbances and make its continued presence in Egypt more difficult.

---

[4] Ibid, p. 93.

Nonetheless, Britain reserved four domains for its exclusive authority in the governing of Egypt. These included: (1) the defense of Egypt, (2) management of the Suez Canal, (3) securing the interests of foreign citizens in Egypt, and (4) the Sudan.[5] The last reservation reflected a growing British interest in the Sudan.

Although Britain maintained a military presence in Egypt, the Egyptian government had a significant degree of freedom to plan and execute policies related to a multitude of issues. Among these were public works and irrigation. Thus, Egypt dispensed with the British advisor to the ministry of public works.[6] Moreover, nationalist forces recognized the potential of their country and were determined not only to gain full independence, but also not to fall under British influence once again. This gained special importance as Britain was still controlling other riparian countries.[7] In time, Anglo-Egyptian relations became strained over many issues, most importantly over independence and the future of the Sudan. However, as the possibility of another world war intensified, Britain attempted to ease the situation by concluding a fresh treaty with Egypt. In this treaty, which was concluded in 1936, Britain agreed, *inter alia*, to redeploy its troops in Egypt and help Egypt become a member of the League of Nations. In return Egypt agreed to the establishment of a British military base in the Suez Canal Zone as well as to provide assistance to Britain in case of war. However, the question of sovereignty over the Sudan remained unresolved. Both countries wished to maintain good relations in the face of possible aggression from Italy, which was on Egypt's western borders as well as on the borders of the Sudan.

The second important British-controlled administration that related to the Nile water issues was that of the Sudan. In 1899, Egypt and Britain agreed to rule this territory jointly, in what became the Anglo-Egyptian Condominium. The agreement resolved the complicated relations between Egypt, Britain and the Sudan. It vested "all civil and military powers in the hand of the governor-general of the Sudan 'appointed by Khedivial Decree on the recommendation of Her Britannic Majesty's Government'".[8] The

---

[5] Collins, *The Waters of the Nile*, p. 147.
[6] Waterbury, pp. 47-48; Collins, *The Waters of the Nile*, pp. 146-47.
[7] Collins, *The Waters of the Nile*, p. 121; Waterbury, pp. 64-65.
[8] Ibid, p. 163.

objective of the Egyptian government and the British high commissioner was, in theory, to govern the Sudan via Cairo. In his instructions to the first governor-general, Lord Cromer referred him to the "big questions," specifically "all such measures ... as involve any serious interference with water-supply of the Nile",[9] leaving the execution of details and day-to-day decisions to Khartoum. However, the reality of this rule was completely different. Once established, the British administration in the Sudan sought independence from Cairo. Indeed, even the first governor-general of the Sudan, General Sir H. H. Kitchener, tended to ignore the British high commissioner at Cairo.[10]

After Egypt won nominal independence in 1922, the Egyptian government inherited this arrangement. However, it was more assertive in claiming its sovereignty over the Sudan. The new ruler of Egypt, Fuad I, proclaimed himself King of Egypt and the Sudan, while the nationalist government repeatedly hailed what it called the unity of the people of the Nile valley, that is, the Egyptian and the Sudanese. On the other hand, Britain sought to consolidate its position in the Sudan and shoulder Egypt out of this colony. An opportunity came to get rid of Egyptian influence in the Sudan in 1924. The British acting governor-general of Sudan, Sir Lee Stack, was assassinated in Cairo. The British high commissioner in Cairo, Lord Allenby, immediately issued an ultimatum to the Egyptian government that included, *inter alia*, the evacuation of the Egyptian army from the Sudan. The Egyptian government was forced to accede, although it maintained its claim to sovereignty over the Sudan.[11] The Egyptian army was restored to the Sudan by the 1936 Anglo-Egyptian treaty. However, the independent-minded British administration of the Sudan continued to rule the country until independence in 1956.

Interests

Egypt's interest in the waters of the Nile has not changed since ancient times. The first real challenge to Egypt's unqualified access to Nile water

---

[9] Ibid, p. 64.
[10] Ibid.
[11] Ibid, p. 152.

came in the Sudan, with the "Gezira Project" in 1904. The project was originally proposed in order to cultivate 500,000 feddans of the Gezira, south of the point where the Blue Nile meets the White Nile near Khartoum. This project was very important to both Britain and the administration of the Sudan. The former saw in the project a way of gaining access to sources of cotton other than Egyptian producers.[12] The administration of the Sudan lobbied strenuously for the project because its own independence required the Sudan's economic viability. The Gezira project represented the only chance to generate economic resources for this, otherwise, undeveloped territory.[13] On the other hand, the British administration of Egypt regarded the project as inauspicious. Not only did it challenge Egypt's monopoly over the Nile's water, especially since the population of Egypt was growing at high rates, but it also aimed to foster competition with Egyptian cotton exports.[14]

Other than the Sudan, Britain had interests in other parts of its East Africa domain. Among the three domains of Britain in East Africa (Uganda, Kenya and Tanganyika), Uganda was most crucial to the flow of the Nile water. At the turn of the century, the Ugandan economy was based on the export of ivory. However, after the World War I, the exports of this commodity fell sharply.[15] Other sources of income were desperately needed. Uganda had the advantage of a traditional central government and a settled population. Thus, Britain experimented with encouraging African farmers to grow cash crops in Uganda, notably cotton. As for the few white settlers who came to Uganda, they mainly cultivated coffee. From the onset, cotton growing was more successful than coffee. The water resources needed for the cultivation of these crops, as well as subsistence farming, which was widespread in Uganda, was not a problem. Uganda enjoyed a high level of rainfall, about 40 to 50 inches per year. This rainfall was also "seasonally well distributed" and was "less variable as well as more abundant" than in neighbouring Kenya or Tanganyika.[16] This allowed a rain-based agriculture that rendered the water resources of the Nile redundant.

---

[12] Waterbury, p. 45.
[13] Collins, *The Waters of the Nile*, p. 117.
[14] Waterbury, p. 65.
[15] Ward and White, p. 144.
[16] S.J.K. Baker, "The East African Environment" in Roland Oliver and Gervase Mathew, eds., p. 13.

What Uganda did lack was cultivable land. Uganda's indigenous population was far greater than Kenya's or Tanganyika's, while its land area was much smaller. This produced a serious problem as the per capita share of cultivated land diminished to a mere 0.8 acres.[17] It was widely believed that Uganda needed an industrial base that would provide job opportunities for its population. A power station on the exit of the Nile from Lake Victoria, at the town of Jinja, was planned to be the catalyst of the industrialization of Uganda.[18] However, the government was short of financial resources and was not able to provide the capital needed to establish an industrial base. Moreover, the industrialization projects needed power sources which required further investments, not available to the colony's administration.[19] Thus, the major interests of the administration of Uganda were land, finance and power supplies, not water.

The British East Africa Protectorate (later Kenya) was much different from Uganda, though it too had little interest in the Nile waters. The colony was sparsely populated and the occupation of the local population was mostly herding, especially the Massai and Nandi tribes, or subsistence farming, for example the Kikuyu tribes.[20] Together, all African tribes did not occupy, or *seemed* not to occupy, a large part of the country's territories. On the other hand, this colony seemed to offer the suitable climate for the settlement of white settlers, which would further promote its economy. Thus, the administration of the British East Africa Protectorate decided to invite white settlers to the colony's highlands. Rain provided for water needs in this area. Only some limited territory in the immediate vicinity of Lake Victoria, originally belonging to Uganda but transferred to Kenya in 1902, needed water from the Nile.

The third East African British colony that was located along the upper sources of the Nile was Tanganyika. The area had come under German rule after the 1890 Anglo-German agreement. The territory was the least populated among the three East African colonies. The land occupied by

---

[17] D.A. Lury, "Dayspring Mishandled? The Ugandan Economy 1945-60" in D.A. Low and Alison Smith, eds., *History of East Africa*, Vol.3 (Oxford: Clarendon Press, 1976) p. 217.
[18] Lury, p. 236; Ward & White, p. 201.
[19] Collins, *The Waters of the Nile*, pp. 211, 219; Lury, p. 236.
[20] C.C. Wrigley, "Kenya: The Patterns of Economic Life" in Vincent Harlow and E.M. Chilver, eds., p. 233.

German settlers totaled merely 1 per cent of the total land available and concentrated mainly "on the lower slopes of Kilimanjaro and in the region of Tanga".[21] Thus, most German economic activity was on the coast and far from the sources of the Nile. Shifting hands after World War I did nothing to change the interests of the colony in the water of the Nile. On the eve of World War II, about 20 years after the British received their mandate over the colony, all the land owned by the non-African population "amounted to less than two and a half per cent of the territory's habitable land".[22] Land ownership was still concentrated in the areas originally settled by Germans, where rainfall was heavy enough to allow rain-based agriculture. Thus, the Tanganyika colony had little demand on the Nile's water.

The Regime

British interests in the Nile were not homogeneous. Instead, each of the British colonies lobbied for its own interests. Among those different, sometimes conflicting, interests, Britain acted as a moderator to achieve the optimum benefit for the Nile regime. On the other hand, with the official independence of Egypt in 1922, Cairo's ability to draft its own policies increased tremendously, especially in the field of water resources. Thus, a partnership was struck between Egypt and Britain whereby Egypt began to shoulder part of the costs of setting up and maintaining a regime to guarantee its share of Nile water. What promoted the establishment of the regime was Britain's interest in maintaining its position in Egypt, its hegemony over most of the Nile valley, and the interests of other colonies along the river. However, the regime was characterized by being reactive in nature. Egypt attempted to maintain the *status quo* as long as possible, and thus discouraged demands by other riparian states. When the need arose and Egypt was forced to address the need of another riparian polity, under pressure from Britain, Egypt negotiated with this polity. However, the negotiations would remain strictly bilateral. The idea of a multilateral

---

[21] G.S.P. Freeman-Grenville, "The Coast 1498-1840" in Roland Oliver and Gervase Mathew, ed.s, p. 450.
[22] Alison Smith, "The Immigrant Communities (1): The Europeans" in D.A. Low and Alison Smith, eds., p. 447.

negotiation involving all riparian polities was rejected by Egypt, as it feared it would increase the demands of other parties.

The first incident in which the British-built regime evolved beyond what it had been came when the administration of the Sudan announced the Gezira Project early in the twentieth century. In the negotiations that were carried out between the Egyptian government and the British administrators of the Sudan, the elements of a new regime were outlined. At first, Egypt resisted this project completely. Not only would the cotton produced from the Gezira project compete with Egyptian exports of cotton, but also it challenged Egypt's claim to the right of full utilization of the Nile water.[23] Moreover, what was extremely worrying to the Egyptian government was that the scheme required the construction of hydraulic projects that would store Nile water, and thus potentially threaten Egypt's water resources. However, the British government was motivated to secure the interests of Egypt, seeking a solution that would increase Egypt's water resources, and therefore increase the cultivation of cotton and satisfy the needs of a growing population.[24] Thus, Britain intervened between the Sudan and Egypt to forge a compromise.

In 1914, Britain pressured the Egyptian government to agree to the construction of two dams on the Nile in the Sudan, one on the White Nile at Jabal `Auliya (to provide Egypt with additional water resources) and the other at Sennar (to provide the water needed for the Gezira Project).[25] Egypt's approval of these projects was conditional on the water allocated to the Sudan not infringing a baseline set by Egypt's requirements at the lowest flood.[26] The baseline was provided by the advisor to the Egyptian ministry of irrigation, Sir Murdoch MacDonald, who claimed that the lowest flood in the century, which occurred in 1914, allowed Egypt enough water while also providing sufficient water for the Gezira project. This argument subsequently became very controversial, and was described by Egyptian nationalists as an attempt to undermine Egypt.[27] Despite the British government's successful mediation of a compromise between the

---

[23] Collins, *The Waters of the Nile*, pp. 152-53.
[24] Ibid, p. 122.
[25] Ibid, pp. 117-18.
[26] Ibid, pp. 119, 123.
[27] Ibid, pp. 120-121.

Egyptian and Sudanese administrations, the outbreak of World War I resulted in the project's postponement.

After World War I and the official independence of Egypt, negotiations over the Gezira project resumed. These dragged on for years and came to a head with the assassination of Sir Lee Stack in 1924. The ultimatum issued by Lord Allenby, that included, *inter alia,* the increase of the planned cultivated land in the Gezira project from the initial 300,000 feddans "to an unlimited figure as need may rise" threatened Egypt's claims for primary usage of the Nile water. This was not in the interests of Britain as it was still genuinely interested in its position in Egypt. Under pressure from the high commissioner, the nationalist government of the Wafd party resigned and was replaced by another, friendlier to British presence in Egypt, that accepted the terms of the ultimatum. However, no Egyptian government, no matter how friendly it was to Britain, could accept the clauses regarding the "Gezira plan." Thus, while accepting the whole of the demands forwarded by Lord Allenby, the new government denounced the Gezira clause.[28] This threatened to cause another wave of nationalist disturbances which, in turn, would have called into question the concessions that Britain won when granting Egypt's national independence. The upshot was that London distanced itself from the "Gezira clause." Lord Allenby now reconsidered his position.[29] He established a commission to decide on the matter. Until a decision was made, he decided to limit the irrigated part of the Gezira project to the original 300,000 feddans.[30]

The Gezira project placed the Egyptian government in a dilemma. Although Britain was pressuring Egypt to accept the project, the Egyptian government could not afford to be seen as flatly opposed, a stance that could not be taken in light of Egypt's standing demand for complete sovereignty over the Sudan--an ambition that presumably entailed concern for the region's development.

---

[28] Ibid, p. 152.
[29] In a letter to the Egyptian Prime Minister Ziwar Pasha, Lord Allenby stated "I need not remind your Excellency that for forty years the British Government watched over the development of the agricultural well-being of Egypt, and I assure your excellency at once that the British Government, however solicitous for the prosperity of the Sudan, have no intentions of trespassing upon the natural and historic rights of Egypt in the waters of the Nile, which they recognize today no less than the past" cited in Waterbury, p. 65.
[30] Collins, *The Waters of the Nile,* p. 153.

Further negotiations commenced between the Egyptian under-secretary at the ministry of public works, `Abd al-Hamid Pasha Sulayman, and R. M. MacGregor, the irrigation adviser to the Sudan government, in 1925/6. In the end, they agreed to adopt an arrangement that would satisfy both Egypt and the Sudan. This agreement recognized "the sanctity of the historic rights of Egypt".[31] Thus, it attempted to accommodate the requirements of the Sudan, *after fulfilling the requirements of Egypt*.[32] The report of this two-man commission, *The Report of the Nile Projects Commission of 1926*, was incorporated into the framework for wider Anglo-Egyptian negotiations on the Sudan's future. These resulted in the Nile Water Agreement of 1929, which affirmed the principles of the report. In addition to recognizing the primary needs of Egypt as the basis of any negotiations, the treaty had other significant consequences. Egypt would provide financial resources needed for the Gezira project. In return, Egypt reserved for itself the right to veto any future hydraulic projects, not just in the Sudan but in all British colonies along the Nile River.[33] The treaty also stipulated that the Sudanese government would allow personnel from the Egyptian ministry of public works to collect hydrological data, and, for that purpose, the government of the Sudan would permit the construction and maintenance of any required structures.[34] The same principle was to be repeated in a subsequent agreement between Egypt and Britain (on behalf of Uganda) to construct the Owen Dam on Lake Victoria.

As mentioned above, Uganda was not interested in the waters of the Nile for irrigation purposes. Instead, it hoped to use the waters of the Nile to generate cheap power to be used for the industrialization of the country and provide employment for a growing population. This scheme was long considered but was not acted upon until the late 1940s.[35] By then, Egypt

---

[31] Ibid, p. 154.

[32] The deal was to provide to give priority to Egypt in the natural flow of the Nile between January 19th and July 15th. After July 15th, the dam at Sennar would be filled up to November, to be used for the irrigation of the Gezira project. For more details about the working arrangement, please refer to Collins, 1990: 154-5 & 157 fn.

[33] Thomas Naff and Ruth Matson, eds., *Water in the Middle East: Conflict or Cooperation* (Boulder: Westview Press, 1984), p. 144; Collins, *The Waters of the Nile*, p. 156.

[34] Okidi, p. 201.

[35] Collins, *The Waters of the Nile*, p. 211.

was more than just formally independent and was assertive in its own hydraulic policies. Thus, to overcome any possible objections from the Egyptian government and the die-hard "Egyptian" lobby in the British Foreign Office, Uganda planned to carry out a smaller hydroelectric project to generate electricity from the natural flow of the Nile at Owen Falls. However, Uganda lacked the financial resources that would to undertake such a project. For its part, Egypt was contemplating the idea of the Equatorial Nile Project.[36] Thus, Egypt was interested in projects to build dams on Lake Victoria and Lake Albert to raise their levels to store water for Egypt's use. However, the scheme involved the flooding of lands in Uganda and/or Kenya. This led to negotiations between Egypt, the Sudan, and the British government, which represented Uganda, Kenya and Tanganyika. The negotiations failed due to procedural matters.[37] However, Egypt and the British administration of Uganda soon resumed negotiations alone. With the encouragement of Britain, the two parties agreed on the plan to build the Owen Dam. Egypt would share in the cost of constructing the dam and provide compensation for the flooded land in Uganda and the loss of hydroelectric power due to Egyptian needs of higher flow rates.[38] In return, Uganda agreed that the level in Lake Victoria would be raised by 2-3 meters and that the Uganda Electricity Board, the authority supervising the dam and power plant would regulate the discharges to be passed through the dam on the Instructions of the Egyptian resident engineer [stationed at Owen Falls]. This arrangement has functioned ever since, even during the most chaotic periods of Uganda's recent history.[39] Again, the regime worked to grant a riparian country, Uganda, limited water usage, with Egypt paying part of the expenses of needed hydraulic projects. In return, Egypt was allowed to supervise Uganda's usage and received guarantees that no future Nile-related Ugandan project required would proceed without its prior consent.

---

[36] The Equatorial Nile Project is a Nile-long project that worked for the full utilization of the Nile's water and envisaged the storage of water in the Equatorial Lakes for the usage of all riparian states, and most importantly Egypt, in addition to the digging of the Jongli Canal to allow the free passage of water from the Equatorial Lakes to Egypt and Northern Sudan. Collins, *The Waters of the Nile*, pp. 198-246.
[37] Collins, *The Waters of the Nile*, p. 220.
[38] Ibid, p. 221.
[39] Collins, *The Waters of the Nile*, p. 222.

Relations between Egypt and Ethiopia were different from those between Egypt and any other riparian state of the Nile river. This uniqueness stems from the fact that until 1936 Ethiopia was the only independent African Nile riparian state, other than the nominally independent Egypt. Ethiopia secured its independence through defeating the Italian invading forces at the turn of the century. However, this did not isolate Ethiopia from power politics in the area, nor from Anglo-Egyptian demands pertaining to the Nile waters. This was translated in 1902 to a commitment by the Ethiopian government not to affect the flow of Nile water into the Sudan without the prior agreement of Britain and the British administration of the Sudan.[40] The first test to relations among the three countries came with the Lake Tana dam project.

Having the Gezira Cotton Scheme as the central developmental project in the Sudan, Britain, or more specifically the British administration of the Sudan, sought to use Lake Tana to store the water of the Blue Nile for usage in the scheme.[41] Egypt opposed the project, motivated by conern over its water supplies from the Blue Nile as well as by its initial objection to the Gezira project itself. In addition, Egypt and Ethiopia were traditional enemies and each was suspicious of the other's intentions. On the other hand, Ethiopia worried about foreign intervention in its territories, and was especially worried about British colonial objectives in the Nile Valley. Moreover, Ethiopia was a feudal society where local chiefs enjoyed large degrees of freedom. Those in the areas where the dam was to be constructed objected to the project. Consequently, negotiations initiated by Britain with the Ethiopian court failed. Instead, Britain attempted to secure the scheme by calling on the help of another European power, Italy. However, since neither European power had actual authority in Ethiopia, the project died until the coming to power of Emperor Haile Selassie.[42]

Even before becoming emperor, Haile Selassie attempted to modernize Ethiopia. As a local leader, he considered the Lake Tana project central to the country's development. However, his efforts were frustrated by the xenophobia of Empress Zwaditu and the leading barons. When he became Emperor in 1930, he sought to breath life back into the Tana Lake

---

[40] Okidi, p. 197.
[41] Collins, *The Waters of the Nile*, p. 159.
[42] Ibid, pp. 159-160.

project.[43] However, neither Egypt nor Britain, representing the Sudan, was now interested. This was a result of a 1929 water agreement between Egypt and the Sudan. Cairo was determined that only Egypt should negotiate with Ethiopia with regard to the Lake Tana dam, a position that Britain, as co-ruler of the Sudan and ruler of other riparian states refused.[44] Eventually, Egypt and Britain reached an accord on the Tana dam project, agreeing to share the cost of the project and divide the benefits among Egypt and Sudan. Both countries proceeded to negotiate with Ethiopia but the Italian invasion of Ethiopia in 1936 terminated these efforts. This marked the first time that Egypt and the Sudan (although the latter was represented by Britain) worked in concert vis-a-vis another riparian countries over Nile water issues.[45] Although the project never materialized, the principle included in the project was to be the norm later, especially in Egypt's High Dam project.

---

[43] Ibid.
[44] Ibid, p. 220.
[45] Ibid, p. 161.

CHAPTER FOUR

EGYPT IN THE LEAD

Britain lost its global stature immediately after the end of World War II. The British Empire had greatly shrunk by the 1950s. One factor that helped to undermine the British empire was efforts by the Soviet Union and the United States to end the Euro-centric global system. The United States pressured colonial powers, especially Britain and France, to grant political independence to their colonies, while maintaining them in the US-led free-market regime.[1] This was related to U.S. efforts to "contain" the Soviet Union. The Soviet Union tried to break this "containment" by providing assistance to independence movements, whether they adopted a Communist/Marxist/Socialist doctrine or nationalistic one.[2] Thus, for different reasons, the two superpowers undermined the colonial system. Britain maintained its presence in East Africa through the early 1960s. At first, East Africa was considered essential for maintaining the British Empire in India and the Middle East.[3] However, with the independence of India in 1948, the end of the British mandate over Palestine in 1948, the loss of Iranian oil fields in 1951, and the total British withdrawal from Egypt in 1956, East Africa lost most of its importance. Britain, nevertheless, stayed on until the early 1960s to preserve the interests of white settlers and to find a formula for granting these countries independence without upsetting the interests of any of the three population segments, the white settlers, the indigenous African population and the Asian immigrants. Tanganyika received independence in 1961, followed by Uganda in 1962, and finally Kenya in 1963.[4]

---

[1] Vernon McKay, "Changing External Pressure in Africa" in Walter Goldschmidt,*The United States and Africa* (New York: Fredrick A. Praeger, Publisher, 1963) p. 102; Peter Woodward, "Rivalry and Conflict in North-East Africa", *Conflict Studies*, No. 199, May 1987, p. 3.

[2] McKay, pp. 98-99.

[3] D.A. Low and J. M. Lonsdale, "Introduction: Towatds the New Order 1945-63" in D.A. Low and Alison Smith, eds., *History of East Africa*,Vol.3 (Oxford: Clarendon Press, 1976) pp. 4-5.

[4] Ibid, p. 63. For a quick review on the independence of Kenya, Tanganyika and Uganda, see: Ibid, pp. 1-63.

By the mid-1950s--and in the context of the Cold War--the Soviet Union established close ties with Egypt, while the United States tried to check Egypt's growing power in Africa and the Middle East.[5] East Africa gained strategic importance because of the importance of the Red Sea to the flow of international trade particularly the flow of oil. The Red Sea was also important because of its proximity to the oil fields of the Arabian peninsula and Iran.[6] Both superpowers tried to gain military bases and facilities in the area, as well as in the adjacent horn of Africa.

With Egypt's Nasserist *coup d'état* in 1952, Anglo-Egyptian relations took a new turn. Egypt began to play a major role in international politics, opposing the anti-Soviet Eisenhower doctrine and the construction of Western defense alliances in the Middle East. This resulted in deteriorating US-Egyptian relations and US opposition to World Bank financing of the Aswan High Dam. Egypt decided to nationalize the Suez Canal and accepted an offer from the Soviet Union to finance the dam. This resulted in the Suez War. With the failure of the British-Israeli-French triple alliance, Egypt gained prestige in international affairs, especially among Third World countries. The following decades saw an aggressive policy within the Arab dimension of Egyptian foreign policy. Egypt also became more involved in global policy making through active involvement in Afro-Asian summits and the Nonaligned Movement. However, Egypt also maintained its interests in the Nile valley, providing assistance to African nationalist movements as well as professional assistance to newly independent countries. The prestige that Egypt gained in the international arena assisted Egypt's role in the Nile valley. Egypt became a major actor, indeed a regional power, in both the Arab World and in Africa during the 1960s.[7]

Egypt's 1967 military defeat by Israel marked the end of an era. Egypt lost much of its stature in the Arab world. However, it remained a major regional actor.[8] Nonetheless, there was a major shift in Egypt's policy away from Africa after 1967. All of Egypt's resources were mobilized to reverse the losses suffered in the war. In the 1980s, Egypt once again turned to Africa, as shown by rising levels of technical assistance to African states

---

[5] Waterbury, p. 107; Naff and Matson, p. 146.
[6] Low and Lonsdale, p. 3.
[7] McKay, p. 84-6.
[8] Waterbury, p. 79.

and increased participation in African politics--culminating with President Hosni Mubarak's chairmanship of the Organization of African Unity twice in the early 1990s. A major limitation to such participation continued to be Egypt's weak economy, which has restricted its assistance to African countries in general and specifically to those in the Nile valley.[9]

The Sudan was a longstanding issue of dispute between Egypt and Britain. Consecutive Egyptian governments refused to discuss the separation of the two countries and linked Britain's evacuation of Egypt to its withdrawal from the Sudan. However, Egypt recognized the Sudan as an independent country as soon as the former declared its independence in 1956. Egyptian-Sudanese relations have passed through many phases since, ranging from warm relations to open hostility. However, relations were never good enough to allow for a "re-unification" of Egypt and the Sudan nor were they bad enough to allow a total estrangement. In 1979, the Sudan was one of the few Arab countries that supported Egypt's peace deal with Israel. That same year the Sudan signed a 25-year alliance pact with Egypt. However, the late 1980s witnessed the return of tensions between the governments in Cairo and Khartoum. Nonetheless, diplomatic relations were maintained and hydraulic technical meetings continued to take place.[10]

Other African polities also started to participate in Nile politics after gaining independence. Ethiopia remained important to the Nile river regime. The country regained independence after World War II, acquiring the former Italian colony of Eritrea with the consent of the great powers as well as the United Nations. This decision lay the foundation for a protracted conflict between the Ethiopian government and the separatist Eritrean forces. As a result, Ethiopia experienced instability until the early 1990s, when Eritrean forces overthrew the government of Ethiopia. During the period when Egypt pursued a Socialist policy and was friendly to the Soviet Union, Ethiopia was pursuing a policy friendly to the United States. On the other hand, when Egypt finally changed global partners and aligned with the United

---

[9] J.A. Allan, "Review of Evolving Water Demands and National Development Options" in P.P. Howell and J.A. Allan eds., *The Nile: Resources Evaluation, Resources Management, Hydropolotics and Legal Issues.* London: School for Oriental and African Studies, 1990, p. 188.
[10] Natasha Beschorner, "Water and Instability in the Middle East", *Adelphi Papers*, No. 273, Winter 1992/3, p. 59.

States, there arose a Marxist regime in Ethiopia that was heavily supported by the Soviet Union.

The three former British colonies on the Nile had good relations with Egypt in the decades after World War II. In the early 1960s, shortly before the East African colonies gained independence, the East African Nile Water Coordinating Committee was established. The Committee recognized that the three colonies were bound by the 1929 Nile Water Agreement, which granted Egypt a veto power over the use of equatorial lakes by the three British East African colonies. However, following their independence, the states of Tanzania, Kenya and Uganda adopted the Nyerere Doctrine, which disclaimed treaties concluded by Britain in the name of colonies. Efforts to coordinate policies among the East African countries produced the East African Community, which did not prove viable. Thus, with respect to the Nile waters, Egypt continued to deal with each of the three countries separately. The same held true with the other three riparian states that were formerly colonized by Belgium; Zaire, Rwanda and Burundi. Zaire enjoyed good relations with Egypt which produced cooperation in many fields, especially in the late 1980s and 1990s.[11] As for Burundi and Rwanda, their demands on the water of the Nile remained insignificant.

Interests

The Gezira project continued to top the Sudanese agenda after the country's independence. It was the major developmental project for the north of the Sudan. As population increased, the aim of the Gezira project expanded from the initial 300,000 feddans to over 2 million feddans. In this project, not only cotton but also food crops were envisaged. The goal was to transform the Sudan into a major food producer in the Middle East. Apart from the Gezira project, livestock activities gained increasing importance in plans for export-led growth.[12] However, additional water resources were needed to undertake the project. Thus, the Sudan attempted to renegotiate its water quotas with Egypt and construct the Jongli Canal in southern Sudan to

---

[11] Ala`a al-Hadidi, "al-Siassa al-kharigiah al-Masriah tigah miah al-Neel" (Egypt's Foreign Policy towards the Nile Water), *al-Siassa al-dawliya*, 120-31, April 1991, p. 125.
[12] Beschorner, pp. 52-3.

bypass the Sudds region, where considerable amounts of water were lost to evaporation. The interests of the southern part of the country in development, previously ignored, gained special attention. However, after starting construction on the Jongli Canal, civil war in the South of the country forced the interruption of the project.

For Egypt, the Sudanese civil war has had a mixed effect. On the positive side, it weakened the Sudanese government which subsequently became more reluctant to challenge Egypt. The civil war also hindered developmental projects in the Sudan, thus limiting its water demands. On the negative side, the war denied Egypt the utilization of the extra water resources that would have become available with the completion of the Jongli Canal. However, Egyptian foreign policy was consistent. Egypt was not interested in the establishment of yet another state that would have its own claims to the river. Thus, Egypt unequivocally supported the Sudan in maintaining its unity, even during periods of bad relations.[13] The Sudan, in turn, never attempted to use the Nile water as a weapon against Egypt, even during the worst media campaigns between the two countries. This was due to Sudanese recognition of the importance of preserving Egyptian-Sudanese coordination on the issue.[14]

The national interests of Uganda, Kenya and Tanzania did not change with independence. Uganda was already beginning a process of industrialization before independence. This trend was further advanced by a growing population and limited cultivated land. However, the hydroelectric power produced at Owen Falls was more than Uganda needed and there was no interest in new projects on the Nile.[15] Kenya and Tanzania also had little interest in the Nile. Until the late 1980s, their agriculture needs were fully satisfied by other sources of water, and their electricity demands were supplied from other sources, for example Uganda's Owen Falls power

---

[13] Osama al-Baz, "Nusanid al-Sudan ka-dawlah lianaha guzai' mina wa ba`ad qiadatiha la tahriss `alaa hazihi al-khusussiah" (We Support the Sudan as a State Becuase it is a part of Us, But Some of its Leadership Does Not Care for This Special Relations), *al-Ahram*, 26 December, 1994, p. 1.
[14] Beschorner, p. 59.
[15] D.A. Lury, "Dayspring Mishandled? The Ugandan Economy 1945-60" in Low, D. A. and Alison Smith, eds., p. 238.

plant.[16] Both countries have been chronically short of financial resources, and therefore have had to delay many development plans, especially in Kenya where using the water of the Nile required its transfer to far away places.[17] However, all three countries reserved their rights for the future utilization of the Nile water, if, and when, the need arose.

Although Ethiopia accounts for about 85% of the Nile water as measured in Aswan, it uses only negligible amounts. The problem in Ethiopia is maldistribution of water resources, with one third of its territory, or 40 million hectares, drought prone while 540,000 hectares are threatened by floods.[18] This has left the country exposed to repeated waves of famine.[19] Agriculture is of major importance to the country, with 80% of the population working in farming-related jobs and 90% of exports related to agriculture. In addition, one of the major interests of the Ethiopian government had been in generating power. However, the power generation schemes on the Nile were proving to be problematic because the 900 kilometers from Lake Tana to the Sudanese borders are too steep, presenting problems in dam-building.[20] The silt coming with the flood waters of the Atbara and the Blue Nile was a further barrier to building dams on the river.[21] Civil war, lack of funds and technological difficulties were the reasons the Ethiopian government did not put into effect plans for Nile utilization drafted by American, Italian and Soviet firms.[22] Yet, the Nile remains the most potential source of development for Ethiopia.

The Regime

It has been shown that Egypt supported Britain in maintaining the Nile river regime, and that by enacting the verification procedures, like on sight

---

[16] Hadidi, 1991: 131; Ahmed `Abass `abdel-Badi`a, "Azzmat al-miah min al-Neel ila al-Furat" (The Water Problem From the Nile to the Euphrates), *al-Siassa al-dawliya*, 145-9, April 1991, p. 146.
[17] Okidi, p. 193.
[18] Beschorner, p. 55.
[19] Okidi, p. 193.
[20] Beschorner, p. 56.
[21] Terje Tvedt, "The Management of Water and Irrigation" in Martin Doornbos et. al., eds., *Beyond Conflict in the Horn* (Trenton: The Red Sea Press, 1992) p. 82.
[22] Beschorner, p. 56.

inspection and international treaties stipulating Egypt's veto over future hydraulic projects, Egypt gained an increased role in the regime. In addition, it was shown that Egypt not only accepted the bigger role, and some of the costs of the regime by financing hydraulic projects in other riparian polities, but also progressively sought a greater involvement. This can be seen from Egypt's demands for strict bilateral negotiations with Ethiopia. Britain was able to restrict the role of Egypt before World War II, but Egypt later pursued more a aggressive policy and inherited the regime from Britain, especially after the 1952 *coup d'etat*. The latter continued to work within the regime to press the needs of its East African colonies, but its efforts to intervene in negotiations between Egypt and the Sudan in 1956-8 were snubbed by both countries.[23] In the modified regime, Egypt attempted to maintain the *status quo*. It also worked to maintain security verification procedures present in treaties signed during the days of Britain's hegemonic role. Using its veto power over international loans, a prerogative of lower riparian states, Egypt approved limited projects in other riparian states when it was forced to address their needs. More recently, Egypt offered other services to members of the regime (for example cheap power supplies) to reward compliance with the regime. In cases when Egypt lost its veto power over financial resources and sensed a threat to the regime, it threatened to use force against any blockage of the flow of the Nile. It also used other tools to exert political pressure, like supporting rebel groups and other enemies of recalcitrant countries.

Using Diplomacy to Moderate Demands of Other Riparian States. Even before Egypt and the Sudan gained full independence, the latter was demanding reconsideration of the 1929 Nile Water Agreement. Sudan's population was growing and areas of the country were uncultivated due to lack of water. Egypt resisted this demand. After the 1952 *coup d'etat*, a new controversy erupted. The Sudan wanted to construct a new dam on the Blue Nile to increase irrigated land. The suggested location was at Rosaries, which was the only suitable location on the Blue Nile in Sudanese territory.[24] On the other hand, the new government in Egypt focused on the

---

[23] Waterbury, p. 72.
[24] Collins, *The Waters of the Nile*, p. 251.

Aswan High Dam, which it saw as the key to Egyptian development.[25] The independent government of the Sudan did not share the Egyptian view, but did not object in principle to the project. However, the Sudan still wanted to renegotiate the water agreement. The Nasserist government proved more amenable than its predecessor to this idea. In the ensuing talks, each party found it in its own interest to accommodate the development goals of the other.

The tone of the negotiations was set by the parties' need for resources with which to construct their respective dams. Egypt sought financial assistance from the International Bank for Reconstruction and Development (IBRD). Because the High Dam would flood parts of northern Sudan, Egypt needed the approval of the Sudan. On the other hand, Egypt enjoyed superior military, economic and political strength, a fact the Sudan recognized.[26] Egypt also enjoyed much prestige in the Third World and was growing into a major regional power in the Middle East.

The Sudan also needed financial assistant to build the Rosaries Dam, and was informed by the IBRD that Egyptian consent was a prerequisite. The country was militarily weak, going through the civil war that preceded its independence and suffering from political chaos.[27] Although geographically the Sudan could unilaterally undertake hydraulic projects to serve its interests, the political repercussions of such a course of action was prohibitive.[28] The Sudan therefore kept Egypt fully informed of its project.

Once the Egyptian-Sudanese negotiations began, the latter urged that it be granted higher water quotas calculated according to land available rather than population. It also demanded relative autonomy concerning hydraulic projects within Sudanese territory, and compensation for the displacement of Sudanese population from areas flooded by the High Dam.[29] Egypt offered to increase the Sudanese share slightly, while maintaining the principle of Egyptian prior needs. Negotiations were broken off many times and hostility increased between the two countries, culminating in the Sudan unilaterally abrogating the 1929 agreement in 1958. Egypt, although eager to start working on the High Dam, had time on its side.

---

[25] Waterbury, pp. 98-9.
[26] Ibid, p. 255; Waterbury, p. 70.
[27] Collins, *The Waters of the Nile*, p. 255.
[28] Waterbury, p. 70.
[29] Naff and Matson, p. 146; Collins, *The Waters of the Nile*, p. 257.

Two trump cards dealt to Egypt enabled it to conclude the negotiations in its favor. With its request for financial assitance turned down by the IBRD, the United States and Britain, Egypt asked the Soviet Union to help it finance the construction of the dam. The Soviet Union was only too eager to establish a foothold in the Middle East. It agreed to extend the required financial resources. On the other hand, the IBRD continued to tell the Sudan that no financial resources would be forthcoming before Egypt agreed to the Rosaries Dam. Thus, in a sense, Egypt had a monopoly on financial resources. The second trump was the establishment of a military regime in the Sudan which was eager to resolve problems with Egypt in order to be able to proceed with developmental projects of the Sudan, stabilize the situation in southern Sudan and consolidate the regime itself.[30] In the summer of 1959, the two countries signed the Full Utilization of the Nile Treaty.

The most important feature of this agreement was that the Sudan accepted the principle of Egypt's established rights to Nile water. Thus, the water quotas of the two countries were fixed at 55.5 billion cubic meters for Egypt and 18.5 billion cubic meters for the Sudan. Although the Sudanese quota was much higher than what Egypt had offered during negotiations, by fixing the quantity in specific numbers Egypt was to benefit from years of higher water levels. The two countries also agreed on how to share water in years in which the level was below aticipated amount. Thus, while any addition in the water levels was in favor of Egypt, the strain to cope with any shortage of water was to be divided between the two countries.[31] However, the Sudan received an important concession: any future project which would increase the amount of annual discharge was to be shared equally between the two countries, which would also share the costs of the project equally. In addition, the Sudan received Egyptian approval for the construction of the Rosaries dam, which allowed it to secure financial resources from the IBRD and other funding agencies.[32]

---

[30] Naff and Matson, p. 146; Waterbury, p. 71; Collins, *The Waters of the Nile*, p. 266.
[31] Collins, *The Waters of the Nile*, p. 270.
[32] Collins, *The Waters of the Nile*, p. 274. As late as 1990s, the Sudan was still not using its full quota of the Nile water. It was Egypt which utilizing the excess water in its own projects (estimated at 6000 million cubic meters per year) (Beschorner, p. 47).

Apart from the Egyptian-Sudanese Nile agreement, there were no other water-sharing agreements among the Nile riparian states. However, Egypt was particularly interested in promoting hydraulic technical assistance and achieving better data gathering regarding the Nile water. Thus, as early as 1960, it accepted an invitation from the East African Water Coordinating committee to participate in the hydrometeorological survey of Lake Victoria. The project was extended in the late 1960s, with Egypt's support and the help of the United Nations' Development Program and the World Meteorological Organization, to survey Lakes Victoria, Kyoga and Albert.[33] In the late 1980s and early 1990s, there were indications that Egypt favoured a more multilateral approach to the Nile water, which represented a departure from its earlier position.

Using Political and Military Power to Prevent Challenges to the Regime. Apart from the Sudan, Ethiopia was the most important actor affecting the Nile regime. During the 1950s, Egyptian-Ethiopian relations deteriorated for a variety of reasons. First, both countries belonged to opposite global power blocks. Second, Ethiopia was concerned over the Arab orientation of Egyptian foreign policy, which it regarded as an attempt to encircle Ethiopia with a hostile Arab/Islamic block. Ethiopia attempted to stem this encirclement by forging stronger ties with Israel, the major enemy of Egypt and other Arab countries. Among all these difficulties in the 1950s, Egypt's proposal to build the Aswan High Dam further complicated relations. In 1957, after Egypt declared its intention of building the dam at Aswan, and during the Egyptian-Sudanese negotiations over the dam, relations between Ethiopia and Egypt degenerated further. Ethiopia declared that any agreement which disregarded its interests would be considered offensive.[34] It also reserved the right to undertake unilateral projects on the Nile within its territories.[35] In 1958, Ethiopia, with the help of the United States government, carried out an extensive examination of the possibility of using the Blue Nile for irrigation and hydroelectric projects. The study resulted in a proposal for building four dams, between lake Tana

---

[33] Collins, *The Waters of the Nile*, pp. 287-88.
[34] Haggai Erlich, *Ethiopia and the Middle East* (Boulder: Lynne Rienner Publishers, 1994) p. 138.
[35] Naff and Matson, p. 147.

and the Sudanese border. However, the program was beyond the financial and organizational capacity of Ethiopia.[36] Moreover, Egypt used its prerogative as a lower riparian state to veto international finances for the project. Despite its friendly ties with Ethiopia, the United States could not finance the projects because it had earlier upheld the veto power of lower riparian states. Egypt nonetheless was alarmed. In fact, this was the worst case scenario that water planners in Egypt often dreaded.[37] Egypt therefore sought to exert additional pressure on the Ethiopian government. One tool for doing so was to support Eritrean separatist movements as well as Ethiopia's enemy in the Horn of Africa, Somalia.

Egypt's support of the Eritrean rebellion was not only motivated by the need to exert pressure on Ethiopia because of its projects on the Nile. It also fit in with Egypt's pan-Arab orientation, as Arab identity was strong among some circles of the Eritrean population. In addition, the growing Ethiopian-Israeli ties were worrisome to Egypt. Indeed, there were proposals to construct an Israeli-Ethiopian-Iranian-Turkish front, backed by the United States, which was clearly hostile to Egypt, which had increased ties with the Soviet Union and the Eastern block. For all these reasons, Egypt tried to exert pressure on the Ethiopian government by helping to establish the Eritrean Liberation Front (ELF) in 1960 in Cairo.[38] The same reasons underlay Egypt's support to Somalia. As soon as it gained independence in 1960, Somalia demanded the Ogaden province from Ethiopia, which the latter had annexed in 1948. This was part of creating Greater Somalia, a major policy goal of the new Somali regime. Egypt's help to Somalia in its confrontation with Ethiopia was clearly designed to confront the latter's threats to the Nile flow.[39]

However, relations between Egypt and Ethiopia were not always conflictual. Both countries had profound interests in African politics and together they worked to build the Organization of African Unity (OAU) in 1963. The same year saw the closure of the ELF office in Cairo. In the mid 1960s, Egypt upheld the decision of the OAU to recognize the existing

---

[36] Collins, *The Waters of the Nile*, pp. 278, 279, 281; Naff and Matson, p. 147.
[37] Collins, *The Waters of the Nile*, pp. 279-80.
[38] Erlich, pp. 137, 132.
[39] Yasser Aly Hashem, "al-Ab`ad al-siaasiah wal-iqtsaddiah wal-qanouniah li-azzmat al-miah" (The Political, Economic an Legal Dimensions of the Water Problem), *al-Siassa al-dawliya*, 210-5, April 1991, p. 152.

borders of states and refrain from altering those borders by force. This implicitly recognized Ethiopian sovereignty over Eritrea. However, the major breakthrough in relations between the two states came in the early 1970s when both powers no longer belonged to antagonistic global blocks. During the short period between 1973 and 1974, Egypt improved its relations with the United States, with which Ethiopia had good relations. As a sign of goodwill, Emperor Haile Selassie invited an Egyptian journalist to investigate Ethiopian plans for the Blue Nile and Atbara. Moreover, Haile Selassie assured Egyptian President Mohamed Anwar al-Sadat that Ethiopia would refrain from affecting the flow of the water of the Nile without the prior agreement with other riparian states. Ethiopia also severed ties with Israel after the 1973 Arab-Israeli war.[40] However, this improvement in relations was brief. In 1974, a *coup d'etat* brought a pro-Marxist government to power in Ethiopia. Thus, a chance to work together on hydraulic projects on the Nile was lost. The animosity between Egypt and Ethiopia returned by the mid-1970s.

The Marxist Ethiopian government of Mengistu Haile Mariam was the most serious threat to the Nile water regime promoted by Egypt, raising the prospect that Egypt might lose its veto over the provision of financial resources to other riparian states. The reason for this was the Soviet Union's disregard for other riparian states when financing hydraulic projects. Egypt itself had received Soviet assistance for the Aswan High Dam, before, and regardless of, reaching an agreement with the Sudan.[41]

Thus, when Ethiopia reiterated its right to unilateral utilization of the Nile in the late 1977 and followed this by announcing hydraulic studies carried out by the Soviet Union, Egypt acted firmly. President Sadat declared in 1979 that any infringement of the Nile would be considered a *casus belli*.[42] However, Ethiopian projects did not materialize, despite rumors of Libyan finances and Israeli technical assistance. Whether Egypt would have resorted to military power if Ethiopia had attempted unilateral hydraulic projects is a matter of speculation. Nonetheless, Egyptian declarations that any Ethiopian action to block the Nile water would be met with military

---

[40] Erlich, p. 173.
[41] Waterbury, p. 71 fn.
[42] J.R. Starr, "Water Wars", *Foreign Policy*, 82: 17-36, Spring 1991, p. 19; Peter Gleick, "Water and Conflict", *International Security*, Vol. 18: 79-112, Summer 1993, p. 86.

force were often repeated in political, diplomatic and military circles.[43] Egypt certainly possessed the means to project its power into Ethiopia. However, Cairo was saved from considering such a costly option by Ethiopia's inability to carry out Nile projects.

By the late 1980s, the Soviet Union was pursuing a global policy of disengagement and therefore providing less support to Ethiopia. Moreover, the central government in Ethiopia was increasingly losing control over vast areas in the country to rebel groups.[44] The civil war drained Ethiopia's resources and blocked developmental efforts in the country.[45] In 1991, it led to the fall of the government. The extent to which the destabilization of Ethiopia was due to Egypt and the Sudan remains a matter of dispute. However, the Sudan clearly helped separatist groups to operate from its territories. Ethiopia subsequently tried to cooperate with Egypt, obtaining technical assistance and aid and securing Egypt's consent, or at least lack of objection, to some minor hydraulic projects. In the 1990s, Egypt tried to meet Ethiopian needs by offering to supply Ethiopia with cheap electricity in return for Ethiopia not embarking on any hydraulic projects on the Nile without Egyptian approval.[46] If Egypt succeeds in securing Ethiopia's consent to this deal, it will have acted in accordance with the Nile river regime and indeed it would preserve the regime against the most serious challenger.

---

[43] *Al-Taqrir al-Istratigi al-Arabi, 1991* (The Arab Strategic Report, 1991) (Cairo: Markz al-dirassat al-siassia wal-istratigia bil-Ahram, 1992) p. 517; Starr, pp. 21-22; Gleick, p. 86.
[44] Lemmu Baissa, "Ethiopian-Sudanese Relations, 1956-91: Mutual Deterrence Through Mutual Blackmail?" *Horn of Africa,* Vol. 13 No. 3 and 4 and Vol. 14 No. 1 and 2: 1-25, October 1990-June 1991, pp. 9-11.
[45] Hadidi, p. 123.
[46] Butrous Butrous Ghali, "Idarat al-mayah fi wadi al-Neal" (Water Managment in the Nile Valley), *al-Siassa al-dawliya,* 116-19, April 1991, pp. 117-18.

CONCLUSION

THE PAST, THE FUTURE

The European scramble for Africa changed the international setting in the Nile valley. When Britain consolidated its power in Egypt, it needed to exclude other European powers from threatening the flow of the Nile water. This was one of the major reasons why Britain established an international regime on the Nile. This regime was concerned with guaranteeing the flow of water. It did not address water usage by riparian polities. Thus, with the establishment of British rule in the Sudan, a new aspect of the regime was developed to guarantee the satisfaction of the need of riparian polities in a peaceful manner. In this regime, Britain acted as a moderator, that is, exerting pressure on all riparian polities to moderate their demands and pressuring Egypt to accept such moderated demands. This was accepted by Egypt because it upheld its right to utilize the water of the Nile and also provided for verification procedures to check on the usage of other riparian states. It also granted Egypt the right to veto hydraulic projects on the Nile. Thus, Egypt played an increased role in the Nile water regime, especially by providing financial resources. With time, the role played by Egypt increased and after 1952 *coup d'etat* Egypt replaced Britain as leader of the regime. However, Egypt's leadership depended mainly on its ability as a lower riparian state to block finances to other riparian states. Egypt also threatened to use military force when it lost its veto power over financial resources to other riparian states. Other actors in the regime complied with the regime because of their need for Egypt's approval for hydraulic projects and/or their inability to generate required financial and technical resources. Within this context, Egypt has been able to maintain the Nile river regime until the present.

Will Egypt be able to maintain the Nile regime in the future? Before attempting to answer this question, it is important to understand how the system is changing. The Nile regime, during Egypt's hegemony, mainly aimed to maintain the *status quo* in order to satisfy Egypt's water needs. In the future, the *status quo* will not satisfy these needs because Egypt's growing population will create increasing demands on the already limited water supply. Thus, Egypt has to think about increasing its use of the Nile water, or alternatively, decreasing its demands. Attempts to use water more efficiently are hampered by the historically wasteful habits of Egypt's citizens. Any effort by the central government to force Egypt's peasantry to adopt new methods of using water resources--by, for example, levying a toll on water usage--would undermine the government. Nontraditional water sources, like desalination of sea water and cloud seeding, are currently beyond the country's economic and/or technological means. This means that in the future Egypt will have to increase its share of Nile water through projects in upper and middle riparian states. However, this option will require negotiations with other countries. And that raises the question of other projects by these same countries to utilize Nile waters on their own bahalf. This is an option that Egypt fears. An idea that has gained wide attention is that Egypt and Sudan might work as partners. In this scenario, the Sudan would become the supplier of agricultural products to Egypt, while Egypt would concentrate more on industry, thus decreasing its water demand. However, this is unrealistic, because it would entail Egypt's dependence on the Sudan, an outcome Egypt would not be willing to countenance. Thus, the long-term future of the existing regime is unclear. What is clear is the necessity of Egypt reviewing its relations with other riparian states.

The Nile regime is also witnessing a change in power structure. As noted before, Egypt depended mainly on its ability to block international financial resources to other riparian states to maintain the regime. Although Egypt's veto power with international financial institutions remains valid, this veto does not prevent domestic financing of hydraulic projects in upper riparian states. In the 1980s, Turkey demonstrated the ability of an upper riparian to circumvent conditionality of international financial institutions when it built dams on the Euphrates with domestic resources. Although none of the Nile riparian states are currently in a position to generate comparable domestic financial resources, this option can not be ruled out in the future. Moreover, upper riparian countries may jointly mobilize their resources to undertake hydraulic projects that would be unwelcome to Egypt.

Without the financial veto, Egypt can only use force to maintain the regime. How relevant will be military force in the future? Egypt remains the most militarily powerful country along the Nile river. It is also capable of projecting its power to the two riparian countries most relevant to its water resources; the Sudan and Ethiopia. However, the use of military force has a high political cost. Thus, while not dismissing the possibility of Egypt using military force if the regime should be threatened, the option would be used only in extreme cases.

One of the most important dimensions of the existing regime has been the low level of benefits accruing to riparian states other than Egypt and, to a lesser extent, the Sudan. The Nile regime, especially during the period of Egyptian hegemony, worked to minimize water demands in other riparian states, thereby putting limitations on their development projects. However, the regime did not threaten existing water demands in those countries. Consequently, the cost of complying with the regime was relatively low and countries did not attempt to defect from it. This will probably not continue in the future. Population growth in upper riparian states increases demands for additional water resources. Moreover, governments of riparian states are increasingly hoping to rely more on irrigation and less on rain-fed cultivation. In the future, this will further increase the total demand of other riparian states for the water of the Nile. Under the existing regime, Egypt would resist such demands, but this would increase the price of compliance with the regime. A point would be reached where the price of compliance would be more than the price of defection. The fall of the regime would follow.

What has so far allowed the Nile river regime to function well has been the relatively low stakes of riparian states other than Egypt and possibly the Sudan, in the Nile water. This encouraged those countries to comply with the regime. Moreover, the Nile river regime was able to establish verification procedures, whereby Egypt, the most vulnerable state to the flow of the Nile, could inspect the usage of upper riparians to make sure that no harm was done to its interests. This situation may be different in the future. Faced with increasing demands by Egypt as well as other riparians, a zero-sum situation, with high stakes to all actors, could arise in the future. Nile riparians may be tempted to act unilaterally to pursue their interests regardless of the regime. Egypt would consider as hostile any action taken by upper riparians to pursue their interests without the verification procedures discussed earlier. High level tensions and possibly military actions could result.

It is clear that conditions are ripe for change. The Nile hegemon, Egypt, will not only witness the waning of its power, but also will lose interest in maintaining the regime as it currently stands. Other countries will also be less willing to go along with today's Nile river regime. What will be the alternative? The future will tell us.

SELECTED BIBLIOGRAPHY

Al-Ahram. "Mushkilat al-miah fi Misr" (The Water Problem in Egypt). *al-Ahram* p.15, 13 March 1995.

Abdel-Badi`a, Ahmed `Abass. "Azzmat al-miah min al-Neel ila al-Furat" (The Water Problem From the Nile to the Euphrates). *al-Siassa al-dawliya.* 145-9, April 1991.

Amer, abdel-Wahab. "Azmat al-miah fi al-sharq al-awsat" (The Water Crisis in the Middle East). Unpublished Paper, Egyptian Engineers Association/Hydraulic Engineers Association, 1992.

Awda, abdel-Malek and Hamdi abdel-Rahman. "al-Ta`awan al-iqlimy fil-qarn al-ifriqi wa haud al-neel" (The Regional Cooperation from the Horn-of-Africa and the Nile Basin). *al-Siassa al-dawliya* 132-44, April 1991.

Al-Ayyubbi, Ilyass. *Taarikh Misr fi `ahd al-Khidiiwii Ismaa`iil Basha.* (The History of Egypt in the reign of Ismail Pasha). Vol. 2. al-Qahiraah: Maktabit Madbouli, 1990.

Baissa, Lemmu. "Ethiopian-Sudanese Relations, 1956-91: Mutual Deterrence Through Mutual Blackmail?" *Horn of Africa.* Vol. 13 No. 3 and 4 and Vol. 14 No. 1 and 2: 1-25, October 1990-June 1991.

Bakr, Hassan. "al-Manzuur al-ma'ii lil-sira`a al-araby al-isra'ily" (The Hydrological Dimension of the Arab-Israeli conflict). *al-Siassa al-dawliya* 132-44, April 1991.

Baldwin, Robert. "The New Protectionism: A Response to Shifts in National Economic Power" in Jeffery Frieden and David Lake *International Political Economy: Perspectives on Global Power and Wealth.* 2 ed. New York: St. Martin's Press, 1991.

Bates, Darrell. *The Fashoda Incident of 1898.* Oxford: Oxford University Press, 1984.

Al-Baz, Osama. "Nusanid al-Sudan ka-dawlah lianaha guzai' mina wa ba`ad qiadatiha la tahriss `alaa hazihi al-khusussiah" (We Support the Sudan as a State Becuase it is a part of Us, But Some of its Leadership Does Not Care for This Special Relationship). *al-Ahram.* p. 1, 26 December, 1994.

Beschorner, Natasha. "Water and Instability in the Middle East" *Adelphi Papers*. No. 273, Winter 1992/3.

Biswas, Asit K. ed. *United Nations' Water Conference*. Oxford: Pergamon Press, 1977.

Collins, Robert O. *European in Africa*. New York: Alfred A. Knopf, 1971.

-------- *The Waters of The Nile: Hydropolitics and the Jongli Canal 1900-1988*. Oxford: Clarendon Press, 1990.

Crabites, Pierre. *Imail al-Muftara `alayh*. (Ismail: The Maligned). Cairo: Dar al-Nashr al-Hadith, 1933.

Crawford, Neta. "A Security Regime Among Democracies: Cooperation Among Iroquois Nations", *International Organization*. 48: 345-85, Summer 1994.

Erlich, Haggai. *Ethiopia and the Middle East*. Boulder, Lynne Rienner Publishers, 1994.

Fueter, Eduard. *World History 1815-1920*. New York: Harcourt, Brace and Company, 1922.

Ghali, Butrous Butrous. "Idarat al-mayah fi wadi al-Neal" (Water Managment in the Nile Valley). *al-Siassa al-dawliya* 116-19, April 1991.

Gleick, Peter ."Water and Conflict", *International Security*. Vol. 18: 79-112, Summer 1993.

Grant, A. J. and Harold Temperley. *Europe in the Nineteenth and Twentieth Centuries*. 6th ed. London: Longmans, 1952.

Guindi, George. *Ismail*. al-Qahirah: Matba`at dar al-Kutub al-Masraiah, 1947.

Al-Hadidi, Ala`a. "al-Siassa al-kharigiah al-Masriah tigah miah al-Neel" (Egypt's Foreign Policy towards the Nile Water). *al-Siassa al-dawliya* 120-31, April 1991.

Harlow, Vincent and E.M. Chilver eds. *History of East Africa Vol. 2*. Oxford: The Clarendon Press, 1965.

Hashem, Yasser Aly "al-Ab`ad al-siaasiah wal-iqtsaddiah wal-qanouniah li-azzmat al-miah" (The Political, Economic an Legal Dimensions of the Water Problem). *al-Siassa al-dawliya* 210-5, April 1991.

Howell, P. P. and J. A. Allan eds. *The Nile: Resources Evaluation, Resources Management, Hydropolitics and Legal Issues.* London: School of Oriental and African Studies - University of London, 1990.

Irani, R. "Water Wars," *New Statesman and Society.* 4: 24-5, May 3rd, 1991.

Khadduri, Majid ed. *Major Middle Eastern Problems in International Law.* Washington D.C.: American Enterprise Institute for Public Policy Research, 1972.

Krasner, Stephen ed. *International Regimes.* Ithaca and London: Cornell University Press, 1983.

Low, D.A. and Alison Smith eds. *History of East Africa Vol.3.* Oxford: Clarendon Press, 1976.

McKay, Vernon. "Changing External Pressure in Africa" in Goldschmidt, Walter. *The United States and Africa.* New York: Fredrick A. Praeger, Publisher, 1963.

Moigne, Guy and Jermoe Priscolli. "Rivers, Water and Mankind: Challanges for the Coming Millennium." Unpublished Paper, World Bank Conference Washington 1992.

Naff, Thomas and Ruth Matson eds. *Water in the Middle East: Conflict or Cooperation.* Boulder: Westview Press, 1984.

Okidi, Odidi. "A Review of Treaties on Consumptive Utilization of Waters of Lake Victoria and Nile Drainage Basins." in Howell, P. P. and J. A. Allan. eds. *The Nile:Resources Evaluation, Resources Management, Hydropolitics and Legal Issues.* London: School of Oriental and African Studies - University of London, 1990.

Oliver, Roland and Gervase Mathew eds. *History of East Africa Vol.1.* Oxford: Clarendon Press, 1963.

Rittberger, Volker; Efinger, Manfred and Martin Mender. "Toward an East-West Security Regime: The Case of Confidence- and Security-Building Measures". *Journal of Peace and Research*. 27, no. 1: 55-74, 1990

Sa`aid, Rushdy. "Mushkilat al-miah fil-sharq al-awsat" (The Water Problem in the Middle East. *al-Ahram al-iqtisady*. March 2nd, 1992.

Shukry, M. F. *The Khedive Ismail and Slavery in the Sudan 1863-1879*. Cairo: Librairie la Resistance, 1938.

Starr, J. R. "Water Wars," *Foreign Policy*. 82: 17-36, Spring 1991.

Stein, Janice Gross. "Detection and Defection: Security 'Regimes' and the Management of International Conflict," *International Conflict*. 40: 599-627, Autumm 1985.

Al-Taqrir al-Istratigi al-Arabi, 1991. (The Arab Strategic Report, 1991). al-Qahirah: Markz al-dirassat al-siassia wal-istratigia bil-Ahram, 1992.

Tvedt, Terje. "The Management of Water and Irrigation" in Doornbos, Martin et. al. eds. *Beyond Conflict in the Horn*. Trenton: The Red Sea Press, 1992.

Ward, W.E.F. and L.W. White. *East Africa: A Century of Change 1870-1970*. New York: Africana Publishing Corportaion, 1972.

Waterbury, John. *Hydropolitics of the Nile Valley*. Syracuse: Syracuse University Press, 1979.

Wright, Patricia. *Conflict on the Nile: The Fashoda Incident of 1898*. London: Heinemann, 1972.

ABOUT THE AUTHOR

Mohamed-Hatem El-Atawy is currently enrolled in the M.Phil. program of the Department of Politics, University of Durham. This work is based on his M.A. thesis in the Political Science Department, The American University in Cairo.

CAIRO PAPERS IN SOCIAL SCIENCE
بحوث القاهرة فى العلوم الإجتماعية

VOLUME ONE 1977-1978
1. *WOMEN, HEALTH AND DEVELOPMENT, Cynthia Nelson, ed.
2. *DEMOCRACY IN EGYPT, Ali E. Hillal Dessouki, ed.
3. MASS COMMUNICATIONS AND THE OCTOBER WAR, Olfat Hassan Agha
4. *RURAL RESETTLEMENT IN EGYPT, Helmy Tadros
5. *SAUDI ARABIAN BEDOUIN, Saad E. Ibrahim and Donald P. Cole

VOLUME TWO 1978-1979
1. *COPING WITH POVERTY IN A CAIRO COMMUNITY, Andrea B. Rugh
2. *MODERNIZATION OF LABOR IN THE ARAB GULF, Enid Hill
3. STUDIES IN EGYPTIAN POLITICAL ECONOMY, Herbert M. Thompson
4. *LAW AND SOCIAL CHANGE IN CONTEMPORARY EGYPT, Cynthia Nelson and Klaus Friedrich Koch, eds.
5. THE BRAIN DRAIN IN EGYPT, Saneya Saleh

VOLUME THREE 1979-1980
1. *PARTY AND PEASANT IN SYRIA, Raymond Hinnebusch
2. *CHILD DEVELOPMENT IN EGYPT, Nicholas V. Ciaccio
3. *LIVING WITHOUT WATER, Asaad Nadim et. al.
4. EXPORT OF EGYPTIAN SCHOOL TEACHERS, Suzanne A. Messiha
5. *POPULATION AND URBANIZATION IN MOROCCO, Saad E.Ibrahim

VOLUME FOUR 1980-1981
1. *CAIRO'S NUBIAN FAMILIES, Peter Geiser
2&3. *SYMPOSIUM ON SOCIAL RESEARCH FOR DEVELOPMENT: PROCEEDINGS, Social Research Center
4. *WOMEN AND WORK IN THE ARAB WORLD, Earl L. Sullivan and Karima Korayem

VOLUME FIVE 1982
1. GHAGAR OF SETT GUIRANHA: A STUDY OF A GYPSY COMMUNITY IN EGYPT, Nabil Sobhi Hanna
2. *DISTRIBUTION OF DISPOSAL INCOME AND THE IMPACT OF ELIMINATING FOOD SUBSIDIES IN EGYPT, Karima Korayem
3. *INCOME DISTRIBUTION AND BASIC NEEDS IN URBAN EGYPT, Amr Mohie El-Din

VOLUME SIX 1983
1. *THE POLITICAL ECONOMY OF REVOLUTIONARY IRAN, Mihssen Kadhim
2. *URBAN RESEARCH STRATEGIES IN EGYPT, Richard A. Lobban, ed.
3. *NON-ALIGNMENT IN A CHANGING WORLD, Mohammed El-Sayed Selim, ed.
4. *THE NATIONALIZATION OF ARABIC AND ISLAMIC EDUCATION IN EGYPT: DAR AL-ALUM AND AL-AZHAR, Lois A. Arioan

VOLUME SEVEN 1984
1. *SOCIAL SECURITY AND THE FAMILY IN EGYPT, Helmi Tadros
2. *BASIC NEEDS, INFLATION AND THE POOR OF EGYPT, Myrette El-Sokkary
3. *THE IMPACT OF DEVELOPMENT ASSISTANCE ON EGYPT, Earl L. Sullivan, ed.
4. *IRRIGATION AND SOCIETY IN RURAL EGYPT, Sohair Mehanna, Richard Huntington and Rachad Antonius

VOLUME EIGHT 1985
1&2. ANALYTIC INDEX OF SURVEY RESEARCH IN EGYPT, Madiha El-Safty, Monte Palmer and Mark Kennedy

VOLUME NINE 1986
1. *PHILOSOPHY, ETHICS AND VIRTUOUS RULE, Charles E. Butterworth
2. THE 'JIHAD': AN ISLAMIC ALTERNATIVE IN EGYPT, Nemat Guenena
3. *THE INSTITUTIONALIZATION OF PALESTINIAN IDENTITY IN EGYPT, Maha A. Dajani
4. *SOCIAL IDENTITY AND CLASS IN A CAIRO NEIGHBORHOOD, Nadia A. Taher

VOLUME TEN 1987
1. *AL-SANHURI AND ISLAMIC LAW, Enid Hill
2. *GONE FOR GOOD, Ralph Sell
3. *THE CHANGING IMAGE OF WOMEN IN RURAL EGYPT, Mona Abaza
4. *INFORMAL COMMUNITIES IN CAIRO: THE BASIS OF A TYPOLOGY, Linda Oldham, Haguer El Hadidi, Hussein Tamaa

VOLUME ELEVEN 1988
1. *PARTICIPATION AND COMMUNITY IN EGYPTIAN NEW LANDS: THE CASE OF SOUTH TAHRIR, Nicholas Hopkins et. al.
2. PALESTINIAN UNIVERSITIES UNDER OCCUPATION, Antony T. Sullivan
3. LEGISLATING *INFITAH* : INVESTMENT, FOREIGN TRADE AND CURRENCY LAWS, Khaled M. Fahmy
4. SOCIAL HISTORY OF AN AGRARIAN REFORM COMMUNITY IN EGYPT, Reem Saad

VOLUME TWELVE 1989
1. *CAIRO'S LEAP FORWARD: PEOPLE, HOUSEHOLDS AND DWELLING SPACE, Fredric Shorter
2. *WOMEN, WATER AND SANITATION: HOUSEHOLD WATER USE IN TWO EGYPTIAN VILLAGES, Samiha El-Katsha et. al
3. PALESTINIAN LABOR IN A DEPENDENT ECONOMY: WOMEN WORKERS IN THE WEST BANK CLOTHING INDUSTRY, Randa Siniora
4. THE OIL QUESTION IN EGYPTIAN-ISRAELI RELATIONS, 1967-1979: A STUDY IN INTERNATIONAL LAW AND RESOURCE POLITICS, Karim Wissa

VOLUME THIRTEEN 1990
1. *SQUATTER MARKETS IN CAIRO, Helmi R. Tadros, Mohamed Feteeha, Allen Hibbard
2. *THE SUB-CULTURE OF HASHISH USERS IN EGYPT: A DESCRIPTIVE ANALYTIC STUDY, Nashaat Hassan Hussein
3. *SOCIAL BACKGROUND AND BUREAUCRATIC BEHAVIOR IN EGYPT, Earl L. Sullivan, El Sayed Yassin, Ali Leila, Monte Palmer
4. *PRIVATIZATION: THE EGYPTIAN DEBATE, Mostafa Kamel El-Sayyid

VOLUME FOURTEEN 1991
1. PERSPECTIVES ON THE GULF CRISIS, Dan Tschirgi and Bassam Tibi
2. EXPERIENCE AND EXPRESSION: LIFE AMONG BEDOUIN WOMEN IN SOUTH SINAI, Deborah Wickering
3. IMPACT OF TEMPORARY INTERNATIONAL MIGRATION ON RURAL EGYPT, Atef Hanna Nada
4. *INFORMAL SECTOR IN EGYPT, Nicholas S. Hopkins ed.

VOLUME FIFTEEN, 1992
1. *SCENES OF SCHOOLING: INSIDE A GIRLS' SCHOOL IN CAIRO, Linda Herrera
2. URBAN REFUGEES: ETHIOPIANS AND ERITREANS IN CAIRO, Dereck Cooper
3. INVSTORS AND WORKERS IN THE WESTERN DESERT OF EGYPT: AN EXPLORATORY SURVEY, Naeim Sherbiny, Donald Cole, Nadia Makary
4. *ENVIRONMENTAL CHALLENGES IN EGYPT AND THE WORLD, Nicholas S. Hopkins, ed.

VOLUME SIXTEEN, 1993
1. THE SOCIALIST LABOR PARTY: A CASE STUDY OF A CONTEMPORARY EGYPTIAN OPPOSITION PARTY, Hanaa Fikry Singer
2. THE EMPOWERMENT OF WOMEN: WATER AND SANITATION INIATIVES IN RURAL EGYPT, Samiha el Katsha, Susan Watts

3 THE ECONOMICS AND POLITICS OF STRUCTURAL ADJUSTMENT IN EGYPT: THIRD ANNUAL SYMPOSIUM
4 *EXPERIMENTS IN COMMUNITY DEVELOPMENT IN A *ZABBALEEN* SETTLEMENT, Marie Assaad and Nadra Garas

VOLUME SEVENTEEN, 1994
1 DEMOCRATIZATION IN RURAL EGYPT: A STUDY OF THE VILLAGE LOCAL POPULAR COUNCIL, Hanan Hamdy Radwan
2 FARMERS AND MERCHANTS: BACKGROUND FOR STRUCTURAL ADJUSTMENT IN EGYPT, Sohair Mehanna, Nicholas S. Hopkins and Bahgat Abdelmaksoud
3 HUMAN RIGHTS: EGYPT ANS THE ARAB WORLD, FOURTH ANNUAL SYMPOSIUM
4 ENVIRONMENTAL THREATS IN EGYPT: PERCEPTIONS AND ACTIONS, Salwa S. Gomaa, ed.

VOLUME EIGHTEEN, 1995
1 SOCIAL POLICY IN THE ARAB WORLD, Jacqueline Ismael & Tareq Y. Ismael
2 WORKERS, TRADE UNION AND THE STATE IN EGYPT: 1984-1989, Omar El-Shafie
3 THE DEVELOPMENT OF SOCIAL SCIENCE IN EGYPT: ECONOMICS, HISTORY AND SOCIOLOGY; FIFTH ANNUAL SYMPOSIUM
4 STRUCTURAL ADJUSTMENT, STABILIZATION POLICIES AND THE POOR IN EGYPT, Karima Korayem

* currently out of print

Discover the wide world of Islamic literature

The journal is produced to a very high standard, and should be a very useful source for all libraries and information users concerned with Islamic issues.
Information Development (London), Volume 7, Number 4, pages 241-242

This journal is doing a singular service to the cause of the publicity of periodical literature on Islamic culture and civilization in all its diverse aspects. Every scholar of Islamic Studies should feel indebted to you for this service.
PROFESSOR S.M. RAZAULLAH ANSARI
President, International Union of History and Philosophy of Science (IUHPS)
Commission for Science and Technology in Islamic Civilization, New Delhi, India

(Periodica Islamica is) an invaluable guide...
PROFESSOR BILL KATZ
Library Journal (New York), Volume 118, Number 21, page 184

Periodica Islamica is a most valuable addition to our reference collection.
PROFESSOR WOLFGANG BEHN
Union Catalogue of Islamic Publications, Staatsbibliothek Preussischer Kulturbesitz
Berlin, Germany

It is recommended for all research libraries and scholars of the Islamic viewpoint.
DR. RICHARD R. CENTING
MultiCultural Review (Westport, Connecticut), Volume 2, Number 1, page 40

You should be congratulated on Periodica Islamica which should prove to be a valuable journal to persons interested in Islam and the entire Muslim World.
AMBASSADOR (RTD.) CHRISTOPHER VAN HOLLEN
The Middle East Institute, Washington DC, USA

Periodica Islamica is an international contents journal. In its quarterly issues it reproduces tables of contents from a wide variety of serials, periodicals and other recurring publications worldwide. These primary publications are selected for indexing by **Periodica Islamica** on the basis of their significance for religious, cultural, socioeconomic and political affairs of the Muslim world.
Periodica Islamica is the premiere source of reference for all multi-disciplinary discourses on the world of Islam. Browsing through an issue of **Periodica Islamica** is like visiting your library 100 times over. Four times a year, in a highly compact format, it delivers indispensable information on a broad spectrum of disciplines explicitly or implicitly related to Islamic issues.
If you want to know the Muslim world better, you need to know **Periodica Islamica** better.

Editor-in-Chief ❑ Dr. Munawar A. Anees
Consulting Editor ❑ Zafar Abbas Malik
Periodica Islamica, 22 Jalan Liku
Kuala Lumpur-59100, Malaysia

America Online • dranees
CompuServe • 72260,227
Delphi • drmanees
InterNet • dranees@klcyber.pc.my

PERIODICA ISLAMICA

Subscription Order Form
Annual Subscription Rates
❑ Individual US$40.00   ❑ Institution US$249.00

Name_____

Address_____

City, State, Code_____ Country_____

❑ Bank draft
❑ coupons
❑ Money order

Expiration date_____
Signature_____

BY PHONE — To place your order immediately telephone (+60-3) 282-5286
BY FAX — To fax your order complete this order form and send to (+60-3) 282-1605
BY MAIL — Mail this completed order form to Periodica Islamica Berita Publishing

SUBSCRIBERS IN MALAYSIA MAY PAY AN EQUIVALENT AMOUNT IN RINGGIT (M$) AT THE PREVAILING EXCHANGE RATE

Subscribe Now! Subscribe Now! Subscribe Now! Subscribe Now!

ملخص

تتعرض هذه الدراسة لاحدى القضايا الهامة التي تمثل تحديا كبيرا لهذه المنطقة من العالم في العقود المقبلة ، الا و هي مشكلة المياه ، و ذلك من خلال التركيز على دول حوض النيل.

يمثل نهر النيل ، الذي يعد من اهم انهار العالم ، اهمية خاصة لمصر. فعلى ضفافه قامت فيها واحدة من اقدم الحضارات في العالم ، و من مياهه تستمد مصر ٩٧٪ من احتياجاتها المائية ، و اخيرا عليه تعتمد ٩٠٪ من الزراعة فيها. و مع الزيادة المطردة في عدد سكان مصر، يزداد احتياجها من مياه النيل في الوقت الذي تظل حصتها منه ثابتة ،الامر الذي سيؤدي الى انخفاض حصة الفرد من الماء فيها الى ٩٨٠ متر مكعب سنويا بحلول عام ٢٠٢٥، و هو رقم يقل عن ذلك الذي يفي باحتياجات الدول الصناعية المتوسطة.

هذه المشكلة لا تقتصر على مصر وحدها ، بل سوف تواجه دول حوض النيل الاخرى التي تحتاج جميعها في المستقبل لزيادة حصتها من مياه النيل لماجهة الزيادة السكانية من هنا كان ضمان وصول مياه النيل ضرورة قصوى تتعلق بالامن القومي لهذه الدول.

في هذا الاطار ، يهدف هذا البحث الى توضيح اثر المياه على العلاقات بين دول حوض النيل من خلال عرض نمط هذه العلاقات منذ منتصف القرن الماضي حتى الان ، مبينا اوجه القوة و الضعف في هذا النمط.

يقع البحث في اربعة فصول. يشرح الفصل الاول كيف ادت التغيرات التكنولوجية في مصر و التدخل الاوروبي في المنطقة الى تغيير رؤية مصر لنهر النيل من مصدر لا ينضب للمياه الى مصدر محتمل للصراع بين دوله.

بعد ذلك ، يعرض الفصلين الثاني و الثالث النظام المائي الخاص بدول حوض النيل ، و الذي قامت بريطانيا بفرضه بداية من عام ١٨٨٠. هذا النظام له بعدان: الاول يتعلق بالعلاقات بين الدول الاوروبية التي كانت تستعمر

منطقة شرق ووسط افريقيا، و هو ما يتناوله الفصل الثاني ؛ و الاخر يتعلق بالعلاقات بين دول الحوض ذاتها، و هو ما يتم مناقشته في الفصل الثالث.
اما الفصل الرابع و الاخير ، فيصف هذا النظام بعد زوال الهيمنة البريطانية و كيف ابقت عليه مصر لصالحها محتفظة لنفسها بدور المهيمن.
و اخيرا تأتي خاتمة البحث لتضع تساؤلات حول مستقبل و استمرارية هذا النظام في ظل المتغيرات التي تطرأ على موازين القوى و على احتياجات مختلف الدول من مياه النيل.

حقوق النشر محفوظة لقسم النشر بالجامعة الامريكية بالقاهرة
١١٣ شارع قصر العيني ، القاهرة - مصر.
طبعة أولى: ١٩٩٦
جميع الحقوق محفوظة. ممنوع اعادة طبع أى جزء من الكتاب أو حفظه بعد تصحيحه أو نقله فى أى صورة و بأى واسطة الكترونية أو ميكانيكية أو تصويرية أو تسجيلية أو غير ذلك بدون التصريح المسبق من صاحب حق النشر.

رقم دار الكتب: ٩٦/٨٢٦٥
الترقيم الدولي: ٩ ٤.٧ ٤٢٤ ٩٧٧

بحوث القاهرة
في العلوم الاجتماعية
مجلد ١٩   العدد ١   ربيع ١٩٩٦

النظام المائي لدول حوض النيل:
١٨٧٠.-١٩٩٠.

تأليف
محمد حاتم العطوي

قسم النشر بالجامعة الامريكية بالقاهرة